The Federal Supplemental Benefits Program

An Appraisal of Emergency Extended Unemployment Insurance Benefits

Walter Corson
Mathematica Policy Research

and

Walter Nicholson
Amherst College and
Mathematica Policy Research

Research support for this paper was provided in part by the Employment and Training Administration, U.S. Department of Labor under contract DOL 20-34-76-12. The opinions and conclusions expressed herein are solely those of the authors and should not be construed as representing the policy or opinions of any agency of the United States government. The authors would like to thank Saul Blaustein, J. Alan Brewster, Mamoru Ishikawa and Tom Joyce for many helpful comments in earier drafts. We owe a particular debt to Jeff Rodman for his background work and research efforts on Chapter II.

The W. E. Upjohn Institute for Employment Research

Library of Congress Cataloging in Publication Data
Corson, Walter.
The Federal Supplemental Benefits program.

Includes bibliographical references.
1. Insurance, Unemployment—United States.
I. Nicholson, Walter. II. Title.
HD7096.U5C65 368.4'4'00973 81-19659
ISBN 0-911558-91-8 (pbk.) AACR2

300 South Westnedge Ave.
Kalamazoo, Michigan 49007

THE INSTITUTE, a nonprofit research organization, was established on July 1, 1945. It is an activity of the W. E. Upjohn Unemployment Trustee Corporation, which was formed in 1932 to administer a fund set aside by the late Dr. W. E. Upjohn for the purpose of carrying on "research into the causes and effects of unemployment and measures for the alleviation of unemployment."

Foreword

Proposals to temporarily extend unemployment benefits have been considered during every recession since World War II. The Federal Supplemental Benefits (FSB) program of 1974 has so far been the largest and most costly of these programs. This analysis and evaluation of the FSB program addresses policy issues currently under discussion in regard to the rationale for and performance of such emergency extensions.

In examining both the specific FSB program and the more general question of whether benefits should be extended during recessions, the authors explore a number of approaches to estimating social benefits and costs. They recommend a cautious approach to emergency extension policies, suggesting that such programs be considered only during especially severe recessions.

Facts and observations presented in this study are the sole responsibility of the authors. Their viewpoints do not necessarily represent positions of the W. E. Upjohn Institute for Employment Research.

E. Earl Wright
Director

Kalamazoo, Michigan
February 1982

Authors

Walter S. Corson received his B.A. from Williams College in 1966 and subsequently did graduate work in economics at the Massachusetts Institute of Technology. Since that time, he has been on the research staff of Mathematica Policy Research, Inc. where he is now a senior economist. At Mathematica, Mr. Corson has been active in analyzing labor and welfare policy issues, and, in particular, he has worked on a number of studies of unemployment insurance.

Walter Nicholson is professor of economics at Amherst College and senior fellow at Mathematica Policy Refearch. He holds a Ph.D. in economics from the Massachusetts Institute of Technology. Professor Nicholson's major research interests concern the labor market effects of public policies. He has published papers on income maintenance and welfare reform, unemployment insurance, and the Trade Adjustment Assistance program. He has also written on more general topics in evaluation research and econometric methodology. Professor Nicholson is the author of two widely-used textbooks on microeconomic theory.

Contents

List of Tables

I. INTRODUCTION AND SUMMARY

A. Introduction

Prior to the 1979-80 recession, Congress had temporarily extended the duration for which individuals were allowed to collect unemployment insurance (UI) benefits in every major recession since the 1950s. In 1970, Congress established a permanent standby program of extended benefits (EB) that automatically become payable during periods of high unemployment. Specifically, during periods when particular measures of the insured unemployment rate exceed certain levels, the EB program increases the maximum duration for UI benefits (including benefits payable under the regular state program) from approximately 26 to 39 weeks. In the recession of the early 1970s, Congress provided an additional emergency extension (beyond EB) that increased the maximum duration to 52 weeks. Later, during the recession of the mid 1970s, Congress adopted emergency extensions under the Federal Supplemental Benefits (FSB) program. That program increased the maximum number of weeks for which individuals could collect benefits from 39 to as high as 52 or 65 weeks. Although it was proposed, Congress did not adopt a temporary emergency extension during the high unemployment period that began in late 1979.

This paper evaluates the overall performance of the FSB program and provides a general framework for future consideration of emergency supplemental benefits programs. It concludes that the desirability of such programs is questionable. On the one hand, emergency extensions satisfy a number of needs that existing policies are unable to meet. For example, they provide increased unemployment protection to workers, and temporarily maintain the income of those individuals who have exhausted their regular UI and EB entitlements. On the other hand, such extensions are inevitably costly because benefits are typically extended in an all-inclusive "shotgun" fashion and may provide substantial work disincentives. It appears then, that with the exception of severe recessions, emergency extensions of the FSB-type should be used but sparingly. Existing regular UI and benefits payable under the permanent EB program should remain the primary means for meeting the needs of the unemployed.

B. Outline of the Paper

The remainder of this paper is divided into five chapters. Chapter II provides a brief historical summary of legislation concerning unemployment benefits duration. It stresses the expanding federal role in such policies and points out the assumptions generally believed to have prompted this expansion. Chapter III briefly describes the characteristics and labor market experiences of individuals who collected benefits under FSB. Chapter IV discusses the general allocational effects of extended benefits programs and examines the specific effects of the FSB program—for example, whether FSB encouraged individuals to remain unemployed longer and how well it maintained aggregate purchasing power during the recession. Chapter V considers the distributional impact of FSB by examining how well it compensated workers for their recession-induced unemployment and whether it prevented poverty among the lowest income

FSB recipients. How FSB relates to existing and proposed welfare programs is also considered. Finally, chapter VI provides an overall assessment of FSB (and emergency extended benefits programs in general) by addressing seven basic questions that policy makers will have to answer in future recessions. A brief discussion of alternative policies during recessions is also included.

C. Summary of Findings

Because this paper is itself a summary of more extensive research on extended benefits programs, it is impossible to mention all of the issues examined in that research. However, some of the major themes, more fully detailed in this paper, are briefly summarized below. First, with respect to the legislative history of UI benefit duration provisions, the following points are noted:

- The debate over the ideal duration of UI benefits is long-standing. Disagreement still exists over how the increased benefits provided by longer UI durations should be traded off against any work disincentives they may cause.

- There is general agreement that the distinction between an "earned right" to unemployment insurance and an income maintenance rationale for benefits becomes less clear as longer UI durations are considered.

- The provision of emergency extended benefits is increasingly regarded as one aspect of an overall federal mandate to provide macroeconomic stability.

- Enactment of the permanent extended benefits (EB) program in 1970 marked the first time UI legislation provided an automatic activation of extended benefits during recessions.

Examination of FSB recipients' characteristics and labor market experiences in chapter III shows:

- FSB recipients were more likely to be women and more likely to be older than other groups of unemployed individuals during the 1974-75 recession. This result stems partly from lower UI eligibility rates among younger workers. It may also have been the result of weaker alternative economic opportunities for women and older workers.

- FSB recipients had, in general, a long record of employment, having worked an average of 17 years, including 5 years at the job held prior to receiving UI benefits.

- Following the layoff that led to FSB, recipients were unemployed for a substantial length of time, an average of 61 weeks during their first completed spell. Three-quarters of these unemployment spells ended in reemployment.

- At a point approximately three years after the initial layoff, 57 percent of FSB recipients were reemployed, with males and younger individuals having relatively greater success in finding work. Real weekly wages on these jobs had, however, fallen by about 10 percent relative to wages on the pre-UI job; nearly one-third of all reemployed individuals experienced a reduction in real weekly wages of 25 percent or more. These declines in weekly wages were about equally attributable to decreases in hours worked and decreases in hourly wage rates.

Among the more important allocational aspects of extended benefits programs examined in chapter IV are the following:

- Extended benefits programs appear to contain work disincentives stemming from the increased unemployment durations they provide. There is disagreement, however, over the exact size of those effects. Some estimates suggest that FSB added about 0.5 percent to the unemployment rate during the mid 1970s.

- The connection, if any, between extended benefits and the job search behavior of recipients has not yet been well researched.

- Extended benefits programs may provide some degree of macroeconomic stabilization during recessions. However, evidence from the FSB program shows that such effects are probably small relative to other stabilization policy initiatives such as automatic and discretionary tax cuts, and that extended UI benefits programs may, of necessity, lag in their impact on the economy.

Chapter V discusses the following income distributional arguments for extended benefits programs:

- The permanent EB program may be sufficient to keep the percentage of claimants who exhaust their benefits within acceptable bounds during mild recessions. It appears that during the mid 1970s FSB reduced exhaustion rates to well below their pre-recession levels.

- To hold the earnings replacement rate (total benefits paid divided by lost after-tax earnings) constant as unemployment rates fluctuate, UI duration should be extended by 3.5 to 5.1 weeks for each 1 percentage point increase in the insured unemployment rate. The permanent EB program is sufficient to hold earnings replacement rates constant during most recessions.

- Antipoverty arguments for UI extensions assume that alternative income maintenance programs do not provide adequate support for UI exhaustees and the need for income support by exhaustees is greater during recessionary periods. Evidence from the recession of the mid 1970s supports both assumptions, although the evidence concerning the second assumption is weak.

- The FSB program had a substantial antipoverty effect, but substantial benefits went to the nonpoor as well. That is, FSB was "target inefficient."

Policy questions concerning UI extensions during future recessions are addressed in chapter VI. Some of the highlights are:

- It is argued that an FSB-type program is not needed during mild recessions because the EB program is sufficient to keep exhaustion rates from rising and earnings replacement rates from falling during such times. Furthermore, the EB program provides breathing space between the start of a recession and the time when further extensions might be needed, which allows policy makers time to assess the severity of a recession and, consequently, the need for FSB.

- Insurance arguments for FSB suggest that potential duration should be increased about 3.5 to 5.1 weeks for every 1 percentage point rise in the insured unemployment rate above the level necessitating the EB program.

Income maintenance arguments for FSB weakly support extensions in the upper part of this range.

- Few options help policy makers mitigate the disincentive effects of extensions. Eligibility restrictions related to the amount of past work experience would have almost no effect on recipient characteristics and post-UI labor market activities. But stiffer job search and job acceptance requirements might have some effect by reducing eligibility for certain groups of workers.

- Several options allow policy makers to target unemployment benefits on the poor, although some of them would be administratively difficult. Use of an income eligibility screen appears to be the easiest, most effective way to achieve this potential program goal.

- Analysis of the recipients' experiences under the FSB program provides little guidance for improving job search outcomes. The availability of employment and training services had few effects.

- Future FSB programs should be financed from general revenues, thereby treating FSB as a countercyclical program and emphasizing that national recessions are a federal responsibility.

- A more generous welfare system would reduce the need for FSB as an antipoverty tool. However, an additional antipoverty effect would be achieved with UI extensions. Income-testing of unemployment assistance benefits for regular UI and EB exhaustees (as recommended by the National Commission on Unemployment Compensation) would reduce the costs involved in reaching that goal.

- Other programs such as a countercyclical public service employment program for UI exhaustees would also mitigate the need for extensions, but they would probably be only a partial substitute during periods when emergency UI extensions were judged necessary.

II. A HISTORY OF UI DURATION LEGISLATION

A. Introduction

Legislators most often take a piecemeal approach to amending social policies, making numerous changes as experience accumulates. UI has been no exception, particularly with regard to duration policy for unemployment benefits. Since the onset of the program, the maximum duration of benefit payments has undergone a sporadic yet continual process of extension, with first the states and then the federal government taking the lead. Although the process has been uneven, several basic objectives have continued to concern legislators and to influence legislation. This chapter will survey these general influences. Three sections provide a chronological history of the duration debate and the legislative changes it brought about. Section B summarizes pre-World War II experience; section C examines the evolution of duration provisions during the 1950s and 1960s; and section D covers the 1970s. Following this brief historical review, we consider two general questions that have influenced duration since the establishment of the UI system: (1) What indicators are appropriate for judging the adequacy of duration provisions (section E)? and (2) How should decisions on duration reflect the distinction between UI and welfare (section F)? Each of these concerns will be analyzed in detail. Later chapters will then emphasize their relevance to FSB-type programs. Finally, section G provides a brief conclusion to the chapter.

B. Early History

The early writings on unemployment insurance established three basic program objectives:

(1) insurance against personal income loss for individual workers;

(2) aggregate income maintenance in the general economy; and

(3) employment stabilization for firms.

At first, the accomplishment of these objectives was limited because of a relatively narrow view of what an unemployment compensation program should be. The program was designed to provide only a "first line of defense" for the ordinarily steadily employed.[1] This belief was emphasized by Arthur Altmeyer, then chairman of the Social Security Board.

> The purpose of Unemployment Compensation is to provide some minimum protection when those persons who are ordinarily employed become unemployed. It is not relief nor is it intended to meet all unemployment under all conditions. The prime objective of Unemployment Compensation is to provide benefits to persons who become unemployed in normal times due to the ordinary changes in business conditions and also to provide the first line of defense during periods of unusual unemployment and severe business depression.[2]

---

1. U.S. Committee on Economic Security report to the President, 1935.

2. Hearing on HR 6635, Senate Finance Committee, 76th Congress, first session, 1939.

Accordingly, the duration of benefits was strictly limited at the program's outset.

> Unemployment Insurance cannot give complete and unlimited compensation to all who are unemployed. Any attempt to make it do so confuses Unemployment Insurance with relief, which it is designed to replace in large part. It can give compensation only for a limited period and for a percentage of the wage loss.[3]

It seems reasonable to ask why an unemployed worker is not covered for the entire spell of unemployment, provided that he or she is actively looking for work and does not turn down any suitable job offers. Initially, there were two reasons for the limit on benefit duration. First was the fear of high costs to the system.

> Coming to the concept of Unemployment Compensation, we regard it as merely a measure to give limited benefits to employees during a period while they have a reasonable opportunity to be taken back within a short time in their old positions. Unemployment Compensation, if it is not to be mere relief, must be based on the contributions that are received. Unless the contribution rates are extremely high, the period during which compensation can be paid will necessarily be quite limited. . . . Unemployment Compensation as we conceive it is something that the man should get in cash during such a period as can be paid for by the contributions.[4]

3. House Report No. 615, 74th Congress, first session, 1935.

4. Hearings before the Senate Committee on Finance, 1936.
"Statement of Professor Witte, Executive Director of the Committee on Economic Security."

These fears were reinforced by overcautious actuarial estimates of the maximum number of weeks of benefits that could be paid for a given contribution rate and waiting period. On the basis of the 1922-1933 statistics, the staff of the Committee on Economic Security estimated that a 3 percent contribution rate could finance only eight weeks of benefits with a two-week waiting period, and only ten weeks of benefits with a four-week waiting period. Using the 1922-1930 estimates for a 3 percent contribution rate, it estimated that twelve weeks of benefits could be paid with a four-week waiting period.[5]

The second reason for limiting the duration of benefits was fear that unemployment benefits posed "economic risks" to the community (Burns, 1949). The payment of unemployment benefits allows the beneficiary to "hold out" for the type of employment to which he or she is accustomed and which is at a wage rate that is "reasonable" (presumably near or equal to that of the previous job). Hence, it may be the case that unemployment benefit payments will permit postponing what may be desirable economic readjustments when viewed by the community as a whole. On the other hand, it is undesirable for the community to force an unemployed worker to accept the first employment opportunity regardless of its nature. There was, therefore, the sense that a healthy economy required having "the right man on the right job" (Clague, 1949).

The maximum duration of benefits then, involved a compromise between the interests of society as a whole and those of unemployed workers. It was argued that maximum duration provisions should only provide for a reasonable period during which an unemployed worker would look for suitable

5. For both estimates the weekly benefit amount was assumed equal to half the prior weekly wage.

employment, and after which the economic risks to the community were too great. This concern was voiced in the first session of the 74th Congress (1935):

> In normal times it [unemployment compensation] will enable most workers who lose their jobs to tide themselves over until they get back to their old work or find other employment without having to resort to relief. Even in depression it will cover a considerable part of all unemployment and will be all that many workers will need. Unemployed workmen who cannot find other employment within a reasonable period will have to be cared for through work relief or other forms of assistance.[6]

C. Evolution of Duration Provisions in the Post-War Period

These two considerations (high costs and economic risks) together with the desire not to make unemployment compensation a relief program resulted in conservative duration maximums. By 1938 only six states provided a maximum benefit duration of more than 16 weeks. In addition, the precise duration for each individual worker was further limited, in all states (except Ohio), through provisions allowing workers to draw benefits totaling only a small fraction of their earnings during a specified previous base period.

The conservative limits on overall duration maximums and the equally conservative limits on individual entitlements meant that unemployment compensation would cover only a small portion of the earnings losses of unemployed workers. Although there was discussion of extending benefits for cer-

6. House Report No. 615, 74th Congress, first session, 1935.

tain classes of workers, there was no consideration of altering durations to meet general economic circumstances. During World War II and through most of the 1950s, economic activity was at a high level and unemployment insurance claims were lower than anticipated. State unemployment insurance funds rose, and it became clear that the earlier actuarial predictions had been far too cautious and that benefits could be paid for longer periods (and waiting weeks reduced). As a result, many states began to liberalize their benefit duration provisions: the average period over which benefits could be received rose from 13-14 weeks in 1941 to 21 weeks by 1952. The increase in the maximum duration of benefits continued through the 1950s in the "absence of any clear norms governing the process" (Becker, 1965). By the late 1950s, most states had adopted a maximum duration of 26 weeks and several states had started to experiment with even longer durations.

Although there were two recessions in the immediate postwar period (in 1949 and 1954), it was not until the severe recession of 1958 that benefits beyond those called for under regular state programs were made available. In that year, extended UI benefits were provided under the Temporary Unemployment Compensation Act (TUC) in states that chose to accept the program. Not all states participated in the program, although some nonparticipants chose to implement extended benefits programs of their own. TUC benefits were funded by repayable "advances" from the federal unemployment insurance trust funds which were ultimately repaid by the participating states. The TUC program provided one additional week of benefits for every two weeks of an individual's original UI entitlement. All later UI benefit extension programs have followed a similar formula by defining the number of weeks of extended benefits to be some fraction of an individual's regular UI entitlement (a maximum in the total number of weeks of benefits that can be collected has also been added to the formula). The variability in the regular UI duration provisions of states has therefore been adopted into extended benefits policy as well.

A second extended UI benefits emergency program was proposed by President Kennedy in the wake of the steep economic downturn in early 1961. This program, adopted as the Temporary Extended Unemployment Compensation Act (TEUC) was broadly similar to the earlier (1958) TUC law. The major differences were that the TEUC program was mandatory for all states and benefits were funded through an increase in the federal unemployment tax.[7] Benefit payments continued to be made through the state programs, however, with state laws determining weekly benefit amounts and eligibility and disqualification provisions. Involvement of the federal government in financing the TEUC program established the precedent of the federal government's taking the initiative in extended unemployment benefits policy and since that time most such policy has originated at the federal level.

D. Extended Benefits Policy in the 1970s

Experiences with the emergency temporary extended benefits programs of the late 1950s and early 1960s led to the recognition of a need for a more automatic policy response to recessionary circumstances. After several abortive attempts at establishing such a policy in the mid 1960s, that need was formally recognized with passage of the Employment Security Amendments of 1970, under which a permanent program of federal and state (50-50) financed extended benefits (EB) would come into effect during periods of high

7. Prior to the TEUC program, several states had adopted extended benefits provisions in their own UI laws. Such state extensions were generally subsumed under TEUC.

unemployment. As with the earlier temporary extension programs, provisions of the EB program allow each claimant to draw additional benefits during such periods up to half of his or her regular UI entitlement, but not for more than 13 added weeks nor for more than 39 weeks in all. For states in which regular benefits can exceed 26 weeks, the state is reimbursed by the federal government for half the costs of regular benefits paid beyond the 26th week during the EB period. The federal share of EB costs is financed from Federal Unemployment Tax revenues and the state share by state UI reserves. These regular extended benefits are automatically "triggered" whenever the insured unemployment rate (IUR) averages 4.5 percent nationally during a 13-week period or when the 13-week average IUR in a state equals at least 4 percent and at least 120 percent of the average of the IUR in the corresponding period in the two previous years.[8] Dissatisfaction with the 120 percent provision of the specific trigger formula has caused it to be suspended temporarily several times. Because of these experiences, states are now permitted to waive the 120 percent requirement if the 13-week state IUR equals or exceeds 5 percent.

There were two temporary emergency extensions of benefits beyond EB during the 1970s. Both were entirely federally financed. The first was enacted in 1971 as the Emergency Unemployment Compensation Act of that year. Under that program a maximum of 13 additional weeks of benefits was payable in states with very high unemployment rates.[9] Originally scheduled to expire in September 1972, the program was continued until March 30, 1973.

8. In computing these trigger rates, national data are seasonally adjusted, whereas state data are not.

9. Because the trigger formula for this emergency program differed from the one used in the regular EB program, the recession of the early 1970s was characterized by the confusing situation that states could have no program of extended benefits, could offer only EB, could offer only the emergency program, or could offer both programs.

It is the second emergency extension of the 1970s, the Federal Supplemental Benefits (FSB) program, that provides the focus of this report. As originally enacted in December 1974 (as part of the Emergency Unemployment Compensation Act of 1974), FSB provided for up to 13 additional weeks of benefits to individuals who had exhausted their EB entitlements (up to 52 weeks in all). As with EB, a claimant's actual entitlement under FSB was set at one half his or her regular UI entitlement. An additional 13-week tier (or another 50 percent of the regular UI entitlement) of FSB benefits was added in March of 1975. This increase entitled individuals to collect up to 65 total weeks of UI benefits—26 from the regular state UI program, 13 from the EB program and 26 from FSB (or up to 2.5 times their regular UI entitlement if that was less). With these provisions, FSB represented the longest duration for UI benefits in the history of the program.[10]

Two further amendments to FSB had the effect of scaling back the program somewhat. PL 94-45 specified that as of January 1, 1976, the maximum duration available under FSB would be a function of the average 13-week insured unemployment rate in each state with an average above 6 percent being required in order to be eligible for up to the full 26-week FSB entitlement. FSB came to resemble the EB program in the sense that it was triggered on (and off) in phases, depending on a state's labor market conditions. In later chapters we develop criteria by which to assess whether these various trigger indicators were set at appropriate levels.

The final major amendments to FSB took effect in April 1977 under PL 95-19. These had two important effects. First, they eliminated the second tier of FSB, thereby reduc-

10. Initially, FSB was financed as a charge on Federal Unemployment Tax revenues. After March 1977, it was financed by general revenues.

ing the maximum FSB entitlement to 13 weeks in states that met certain trigger requirements, and they provided for the ultimate phaseout of the FSB program in early 1978. Second, and perhaps more important, the amendments mandated, for the first time, that certain uniform federal eligibility and disqualification standards would apply to FSB recipients. The previous practice had been to use existing state standards. The federal standards were generally more stringent than the corresponding state standards and were enacted in part because of congressional desire to "tighten-up" the FSB program. The provisions seem to have had that effect, since FSB denials increased sharply following implementation of the new standards, and apparently many FSB claimants stopped filing on their own once they learned of the new requirements.

Overall then, the 1970s experienced major changes in extended UI benefits policy. The EB program was established as a permanent, automatic UI policy response to recessions, and a variety of emergency legislation was enacted that provided further temporary extensions. In the recession of 1979-1980, the EB program also came into effect in many states and, for a while, on a national basis, although after considerable congressional debate no emergency extension program was enacted. Before turning to a substantive examination of the most important piece of emergency legislation during the 1970s (the FSB program), it may be helpful to provide a brief review of some major policy issues that have characterized virtually every debate over emergency benefit extensions.

E. Indicators for Legislative Action: Unemployment and Exhaustion Rates

Certain regularities are apparent in the legislative debates about emergency extensions of UI benefit durations. We will focus on two: indicators of the need for extended benefits, and the relationship between UI and welfare. With respect to the first, there is general agreement on the kinds of economic indicators that tend to signal the need for emergency action on extended benefits. Throughout the post-World War II period, three macroeconomic variables have played an important role in influencing legislative decisions: the overall unemployment rate, the mean (or median) duration of unemployment spells, and the exhaustion rate for regular UI. Table II.1 shows that these three measures are closely related for the 1953-1978 period.[11] Quarterly data on the median duration of unemployment spells and the exhaustion rate for regular UI were used as dependent variables in simple regressions run with the overall unemployment rate as the sole explanatory variable. These simple regressions explained the variance of the dependent variable quite well—85 percent of the variance in spell durations and 92 percent of the variance in exhaustion rates were explained by a single measure of labor market tightness—the overall unemployment rate. More specifically, the results show that each 1 percentage point increase in the unemployment rate tends to be correlated with a nearly one-week (0.93) increase in the length of the median unemployment spell. Since the national unemployment rate increases by 2 or 3 percentage points during a "typical" economic downturn, these results indicate that the median worker is unemployed about two or three weeks longer during such periods. The incidence of relatively long unemployment spells also increases commensurately. Table II.1 also shows that higher unemployment rates are associated with higher rates of regular UI benefit exhaustion. On average, each 1 percentage point rise in the unemployment rate tends to be associated with a 4.4 percentage point increase in the exhaustion rate. Therefore, ex-

11. Underlying data on these variables for the 1974-77 period are provided in tables V.1 and V.2.

haustion rates for regular UI might rise by about 9 to 13 percentage points (say from 25 to 35+ percent) during a typical downturn. Each of these empirical regularities has been reflected in legislative debates.

TABLE II.1

Effect of Unemployment Rate on Duration of Unemployment Spell and UI Exhaustion Rate United States, 1953-1978[a]

Independent Variable	Dependent Variables	
Measure of Effect of Unemployment Rate[b]	Median Duration of Unemployment Spell	Exhaustion Rate for Regular UI
Coefficient	0.934	4.42
(t statistic)	(9.692)	(11.493)
Constant	-0.060	6.13
(t statistic)	(-0.108)	(3.740)
R^2	.847	.922
Standard Error	0.697	.028
F-Statistic	108.157	148.147
Durbin Watson Statistic	2.11	2.077

a. Sources of the data underlying these measures are *Unemployment Insurance Statistics* (various issues) for the exhaustion rate series and *Employment and Earnings* (various issues) for the other data.

b. Seasonally adjusted quarterly rates.

The connection between rising unemployment and lengthening unemployment spells was clearly reflected by Secretary of Labor John T. Dunlop's statement before the Senate Finance Committee in 1975:

> I do think that it is appropriate that the duration should rise in times of very heavy unemployment.

> The reason for that principle, I think is this: the job search which takes place in a labor market may take a lot longer, and one may have to travel a lot further in times in which unemployment levels are appreciably higher. So, the notion of expanding the benefits, with the level of unemployment is, on the whole, a sound principle.[12]

The concern over longer unemployment spells during periods of high unemployment also leads naturally to consideration of UI exhaustion rates. If, in times of high unemployment, benefit duration should increase to provide "adequate" coverage for those workers whose unemployment spells lengthen, the exhaustion rate is then a "test" by which the adequacy of benefit durations might be judged. In 1958, for example, President Eisenhower, in a message to Congress, called for legislation extending benefits for those workers who had exhausted their regular benefits. In reference to the President's remarks, Secretary of Labor James P. Mitchell stated in Senate hearings before the Finance Committee:

> The President's recommendation for this temporary legislation was based on the fact not only that unemployment increased sharply after the first of the year and rose to heights far above normal, but also that the rate at which unemployed workers were exhausting their unemployment insurance benefits and still remained unemployed was sharply increasing in many areas.[13]

The belief of the founders of the unemployment insurance system—that the duration of benefits should be sufficient to

12. Senate Hearings (Finance Committee) 94th Congress, first session, June 1975.

13. Senate Hearings (Finance Committee) 85th Congress, second session, 1958.

insure protection through temporary periods of unemployment—has generally been interpreted to mean "a duration sufficient to enable the majority or the 'great majority' of insured workers to find suitable work before exhausting their benefit rights."[14] Although there has been little explicit agreement as to what the "great majority" of workers should mean, in practice the notion has been widely held that total exhaustion rates for all UI benefits (including extensions) should not rise precipitously during recessions. In chapters IV and V we will examine the connection between the length of unemployment spells, exhaustion rates, and UI extensions in considerably more detail, and the empirical results indicated in table II.1 will provide some useful rules of thumb for discussing policy alternatives.

F. Unemployment Insurance and Welfare

Another recurrent issue in the legislative debate over extensions in UI duration is differentiating between an unemployment insurance and a welfare rationale for compensating individuals with very long unemployment spells. The link between the insurable risk of unemployment and the cause of the present unemployment becomes unclear during longer spells. Several observers have suggested that after a worker has exhausted a certain number of weeks of benefits, he or she should no longer be the responsibility of the unemployment insurance system but should instead become the responsibility of the welfare system. In some European countries, for example, income-tested welfare payments automatically become payable after exhaustion of regular unemployment insurance benefits. Recent proposals in this country have suggested similar arrangements, or have at least attempted to define more clearly a workable relation-

14. "The Role of Unemployment Resources Today . . . And Tomorrow," *Employment Security Review*, August 1962, p. 33.

ship between unemployment insurance and income maintenance programs. Former Secretary of Labor Dunlop, in the same statement in which he advocated increasing benefit durations during the 1974-75 recession, also spoke of the need to limit the extensions:

> I cannot tell you where my ideal limit is. I, myself, am concerned . . . about our system degenerating into what I call a public assistance program. . . . I do favor this extension at this time because we have not in this country placed into effect a comprehensive type of welfare program; [Another] solution to these two problems would say after a certain point a person who was unemployed—I do not care for the moment whether you say 52 weeks, 65 weeks, 78 weeks, or some other number—ought to be treated financially not as part of the unemployment insurance system, financed in the way an unemployment insurance system is, but ought to be treated as a part of some welfare program.[15]

Dunlop went on to speak of the very same "economic risks" that were responsible for the limits on the duration of benefits at the outset of the UI program. He noted that unemployment durations of 52 weeks or more may be due to some structural factor in the community and/or industry that would result in the lost jobs never again becoming available. In such circumstances, direct income support may be more appropriate than continuing unemployment insurance benefits.

Debate over the connection between UI extensions and public assistance continues to this day. Two general ques-

15. Senate Hearings (Finance Committee) 94th Congress, first session, June 1975.

tions have characterized more recent discussions of the subject: (1) whether extended UI benefits should be subject to some type of means test; and (2) how extensions should be financed. Although there has been considerable analysis of the first question (and we take up the issue in detail in chapter V), it has received only slight attention in legislative debate. Emergency extensions have usually been enacted quite rapidly leaving little time for a full airing of the means-testing issue. There have been, however, some changes in the financing arrangements considered appropriate for emergency extensions. After March 1977, FSB benefits were financed through general revenues and this represented the first departure from exclusive use of UI tax revenues for UI benefits. Implicit in this decision to finance FSB through general revenues was the recognition that such long term benefits should not be considered an appropriate financial responsibility of UI tax-paying employers within the traditional social insurance framework. Rather, payment of emergency extended benefits should be regarded as part of the more general responsibility of the federal government for macroeconomic activity.

G. Conclusion

This brief history of the legislative debate over UI duration provisions clearly illustrates two points. First, the debate is longstanding. Many of the basic issues addressed in the formative stages of the UI system remain as controversial today as they were then. What the duration of UI benefits should be and how that duration should be altered during recession is simply not agreed upon. Second, extended benefit policy has become increasingly a federal responsibility. As the federal government has taken a greater role in the maintenance of overall economic activity, it has come also to accept responsibility for initiating compensation programs, such as UI extensions. This is reflected both in the permanent EB program (required in all states and half federally financed) that is automatically "triggered" during recessions, and in the emergency programs that have been entirely federally financed and structured by federal policy makers. This increased responsibility at the federal level heightens the need to coordinate extended UI benefits policy with other federal programs.

III. LABOR MARKET EXPERIENCES AND CHARACTERISTICS OF FSB RECIPIENTS

A. Introduction

This chapter provides background information for our evaluation of the FSB program. It describes the demographic and pre-UI employment characteristics of FSB recipients, and it also describes their labor market experiences during and after receipt of UI benefits. Data for this chapter and much of the analysis reported in subsequent chapters were collected for a sample of FSB recipients in 15 selected states; the sample was chosen to represent the 2.8 million recipients who began collecting FSB during 1975.[1] Whenever possible, these recipients and their experiences were compared to other unemployed groups. These comparison groups included individuals who collected Extended Benefits and not FSB in 1975, and long term unemployed individuals who had lost their jobs.[2]

1. A complete description of this sample and more extensive analyses of the data can be found in Corson, et al. (1977) and Brewster, et al. (1978). The first of these reports was based on data collected for a sample of 6,835 FSB recipients who were interviewed in March of 1976. A second interview was conducted in November 1977 with a subsample of 1,522 of these individuals; this smaller sample was used for the second report. This chapter draws heavily on chapter II of the first report, which was written by Valerie Leach and on chapter II of the second report, which was written by Walter Nicholson.

2. EB recipient data were obtained from the same survey as the data for FSB recipients. Data for long term unemployed job losers were obtained from special tabulations from the March 1975 Current Population Survey.

B. Demographic and Pre-UI Employment Characteristics of FSB Recipients

Demographic Characteristics

Compared with EB recipients, or job losers who had been unemployed for 27 weeks or longer, FSB recipients were more likely to be female. Women accounted for 48 percent of FSB recipients, whereas less than 40 percent of the regular insured unemployed and of the long term unemployed job losers[3] and not quite 44 percent of EB recipients were female.

FSB recipients also tended to be older than other unemployed groups—their mean age was 40 years, compared with a mean age of 36 for EB recipients, and 38 for job losers unemployed 27 weeks or more. Twenty-three percent of all FSB men and 21 percent of FSB women were 55 years old or older. These percentages were significantly higher than the analogous figures for EB recipients (13 percent of each sex group).[4] Older men also formed a larger proportion of the male FSB population than of male long term unemployed job losers.

The relatively higher incidence of women and of older workers among beneficiaries of extended unemployment insurance programs and among exhaustees of regular UI programs compared with other groups in the labor force also has been noted in other studies.[5] It stems partly from lower UI eligibility rates among younger workers and may also be due to weaker alternative economic opportunities for women and for older workers.

3. The long term unemployed are defined here as those who had been unemployed 27 weeks or longer. See table III.1.

4. Differences are termed significant in this chapter if they are statistically significant at the 95 percent confidence level.

5. See, for example, Nicholson and Corson (1976).

The proportions of white and nonwhite workers among female FSB recipients were the same as among female long term job losers. However, there was a higher proportion of whites among FSB males than among male long term job losers. This is partly due to the lower age of minority male workers, compared with their white counterparts, and to the lower UI eligibility rates of younger workers.

The education levels of FSB recipients were, on average, comparable with those of other groups unemployed for 27 weeks or more. Over 60 percent of them had some high school education or had graduated from high school but had no further education. Levels of education, however, varied more among FSB recipients than among other comparison groups—relatively more of them had no high school education and a higher proportion of them had some college education. The contrast was greatest in comparison with EB recipients. This difference between EB and FSB recipients was associated with differences in their occupations and industries. As we show in the next section, proportionately more EB than FSB recipients were employed in manufacturing industries, where employees tend to have some high school but no higher level of education.

Sixty-one percent of FSB recipients (65 percent of the women and 57 percent of the men) were married and headed, or shared responsibility for heading, their families; whereas only 49 percent of all long term unemployed job losers (55 percent of the women and 45 percent of the men) were from husband-wife headed families. Almost one-third of the job loser group lived with but did not head their families, compared with only 18 percent of FSB recipients. Among the men in the job loser and FSB recipient groups, the family nonhead proportions were 40 and 24 percent, respectively; among the women, they were 19 and 12 percent, respectively.

TABLE III.1

Demographic Characteristics of FSB Recipients and Job Losers Unemployed 27 Weeks or More

Demographic Characteristic	FSB Recipients			Job Losers Unemployed 27 Weeks or Longer		
	Total	Male	Female	Total	Male	Female
Age						
Under 25	21.2%	25.2%	16.9%	23.5%	26.0%	19.3%
25 - 34	25.3	24.7	25.9	22.8	25.3	18.5
35 - 44	15.4	13.2	17.8	17.5	18.6	15.7
45 - 54	16.3	14.1	18.7	17.6	14.8	22.3
55 - 64	13.5	13.8	13.1	15.9	14.4	18.6
65 and Older	8.3	8.9	7.5	2.7	0.9	5.6
Total	100.0%	100.0%	100.0%	100.0%	100.0%	100.0%
Mean Age	39.7	39.1	40.4	38.4	36.6	41.5
Race						
White	84.7%	83.0%	86.7%	79.0%	74.6%	86.6%
Black and Other	15.2	17.0	13.2	21.0	25.4	13.4
Total	100.0%	100.0%	100.0%	100.0%	100.0%	100.0%
Education						
Some Elementary School	8.7%	10.0%	7.1%	10.4%	11.1%	9.2%
Completed Elementary School	8.3	9.5	7.0	8.0	8.2	7.7

Some High School	23.8	23.2	24.4	26.2	28.5	22.4
High School Graduate	38.5	32.9	44.5	40.7	35.4	49.9
Some College	15.4	17.6	13.0	10.0	11.0	8.3
College Graduate	5.5	6.9	4.0	4.7	5.8	2.6
Total	100.0%	100.0%	100.0%	100.0%	100.0%	100.0%
Mean Years of School Completed	11.2	11.1	11.2	10.7	10.7	10.8
Family Type and Position of Recipient						
Husband-Wife Headed Family						
Husband	30.0%	57.1%	n.a.	28.4%	44.8%	n.a.
Wife	31.1	n.a.	65.4%	20.3	n.a.	55.3%
Other Family Head	6.2	2.9	9.8	6.8	3.2	13.0
Unrelated Individual (Not Living with Family)	14.6	16.0	13.1	12.4	12.4	12.5
Nonhead Family Member	18.2	24.0	11.7	32.2	39.7	19.2
Total	100.0%	100.0%	100.0%	100.0%	100.0%	100.0%
Weighted Sample Size	6,817	3,579	3,238	4,200	2,600	1,600

SOURCE: FSB data are weighted observations from the initial FSB/SUA survey. (See Corson et al., 1977). Data on job losers were obtained from special tabulations from the public use file of the Current Population Survey, March 1975.

NOTES: Distribution may not sum to total becuase of rounding: n.a. = not applicable.

Pre-UI Employment Characteristics

The industries in which FSB and EB recipients and all long term unemployed job losers had been employed are reported in table III.2. The high rate of UI coverage among employees of most manufacturing firms is reflected in the relatively large proportion of FSB and EB recipients who had worked in these industries. However, fewer FSB than EB males were employed in durable goods manufacturing—27 percent compared with 38 percent—and fewer FSB than EB females worked in nondurable goods manufacturing—27 percent compared with 35 percent. Altogether, 44 percent of FSB recipients worked in manufacturing industries. The lower proportion of FSB compared with EB recipients (53 percent) from manufacturing industries may have been the result of manufacturing firms recalling employees when the economy started to recover. Relatively more EB recipients were recalled to their pre-UI jobs and did not collect unemployment insurance long enough to begin collecting FSB.

FSB recipients held their pre-UI jobs for an average of about five years, and worked an average of about 26 months during the three years before claiming UI (see table III.3). EB recipients, especially the men—possibly because they were younger, on average—had not held their pre-UI jobs so long.

Mean weekly earnings of FSB recipients were generally slightly lower than the national average for production and nonsupervisory workers within the same industry, as were their hours of work. However, the relatively high proportion of FSB recipients from manufacturing resulted in their overall average earnings being higher than the national average for production and nonsupervisory workers. Only slightly fewer FSB than EB males belonged to a union—42 percent compared with 45 percent.

TABLE III.2

Percentage Distribution of FSB and EB Recipients and of Job Losers Unemployed 27 Weeks or Longer, by Industry and Sex[a]

Industry	FSB Recipients			EB Recipients			Job Losers Unemployed 27 Weeks or Longer		
	Total	Male	Female	Total	Male	Female	Total	Male	Female
Agriculture, Forestry, Fisheries	0.7%	1.1%	0.3%	0.3%	0.0%	0.0%	1.2%	1.5%	0.8%
Mining	0.3	0.5	0.1	0.5	0.7	0.3	0.3	0.5	0.0
Construction	10.6	18.7	1.6	11.3	19.6	0.5	12.5	18.6	1.7
Durable Goods Manufacturing	24.0	27.4	20.2	30.7	37.8	21.5	20.0	19.6	20.5
Nondurable Goods Manufacturing	20.1	14.2	26.7	22.2	12.3	35.3	14.9	11.9	20.2
Transportation and Public Utilities	4.7	5.7	3.7	4.2	5.4	2.5	4.7	6.3	1.9
Wholesale Trade	2.6	2.4	2.8	1.4	1.5	1.3	3.3	3.6	2.8
Retail Trade	15.5	11.0	20.5	12.6	8.5	17.8	19.5	16.7	24.5
Services	17.1	12.5	22.2	13.1	8.6	18.8	22.0	18.8	27.7

Local Government Administration	0.3	0.3	0.3	0.3	0.3	0.4	1.6	2.5	0.0
State and Federal Government Administration	4.1	6.3	1.5	3.4	4.7	1.6			
Total	100.0%	100.0%	100.0%	100.0%	100.0%	100.0%	100.0%	100.0%	100.0%
Weighted Sample Size	6,819	3,577	3,242	1,021	573	448	4,200	2,600	1,600

SOURCE: FSB and EB data are weighted observations from the initial FSB/SUA survey. Data for job losers were obtained from special tabulations from the public use file of the Current Population Survey, March 1975.

NOTE: Distribution may not sum to total because of rounding.

a. Industry refers to the job held prior to spell of unemployment. For FSB and EB recipients, this job, the "pre-UI" job, was the longest job during the twelve months prior to claiming unemployment insurance.

TABLE III.3

Pre-UI Employment Characteristics of FSB and EB Recipients

Pre-UI	FSB Recipients			EB Recipients		
Employment Characteristic	Total	Male	Female	Total	Male	Female
Mean Number of Years Since First Regular Job	20.0	20.8	19.2	16.5	16.8	16.4
Mean Percentage of Years Worked Since Then	83.5	89.1	77.1	88.2	90.3	85.4
Mean Number of Months Worked in 3 Years Prior to Claim for Unemployment Compensation	25.8	26.8	24.8	27.0	27.8	26.2
Mean Number of Months Between Start and End Date of Pre-UI Job	60.9	63.7	57.9	52.4	50.0	56.2
Mean Gross Weekly Earnings in Pre-UI Job[a]	$170	$199	$139	$167	$208	$116
Mean Hours Worked per Week in Pre-UI Job	40.4	42.3	38.2	40.6	42.7	37.9
Percentage Belonging to a Labor Union in Pre-UI Job	35.4	42.3	27.7	36.8	45.0	26.6
Weighted Sample Size	6,099	3,234	2,864	1,009	563	445

SOURCE: Data are weighted observations from the initial FSB/SUA survey.

a. Adjusting pre-UI weekly earnings to 1975 dollars yielded the following results:

FSB Recipients			EB Recipients		
Total	Male	Female	Total	Male	Female
$180	$210	$147	$173	$215	$120

C. Labor Market Experiences of FSB Recipients Following Their Initial Layoff

Labor Market Experiences Over Time

Data from the FSB surveys enable us to examine the labor market experiences of FSB recipients during approximately three years, beginning with the start of their UI claim (usually late 1974 or early 1975) and ending with the November 1977 interviews. During this time (see table III.4) unemployment was the predominant status for all groups of recipients except young males (under age 25), who spent more time employed than unemployed, and older females (age 65 and over), who spent the majority of their time out of the labor force. Overall, FSB recipients spent nearly half the time unemployed.[6] The implied unemployment rate was 59 percent over the entire three-year period. That is, FSB recipients who were in the labor force during that period were unemployed 59 percent of the time. With the exception of young males, all age-sex groups had unemployment rates over 50 percent. The highest rates were experienced by older respondents, both male and female. Other data from the survey show that respondents collected UI benefits, including FSB, for an average of 53 weeks over this period. Because unemployment averaged about 78 weeks during the period, we can conclude that about 68 percent of all the unemployment experienced by FSB recipients was covered by unemployment benefits.

More than three-quarters of the weeks of unemployment experienced by FSB recipients over the three-year period discussed above occurred during the first completed spell that started at the initial UI claim date and ended before

6. An individual was characterized as unemployed if s/he was out of work and looking for a job, or awaiting recall—a situation that generally did not apply to FSB recipients.

TABLE III.4

Percentage Distribution, by Labor Force Status, of Time from Initial UI Claim Date to November 1977 for FSB Recipients, by Age and Sex

(Total Weeks)

Sex and Age	Sample Size	Labor Force Status: Employed	Unemployed	Out Of Labor Force	Total
TOTAL	1,350	34.4%	49.4%	16.3%	100.0%
MALE					
Total	690	38.7	50.0	11.4	100.0
Under 25	176	48.3	46.3	5.4	100.0
25-34	161	46.9	49.2	4.0	100.0
35-44	104	42.2	53.6	4.2	100.0
45-54	92	36.1	53.9	10.0	100.0
55-64	98	24.9	48.8	26.3	100.0
65 and over	59	8.0	52.7	39.4	100.0
FEMALE					
Total	660	29.7	48.8	21.5	100.0
Under 25	108	36.8	42.7	20.6	100.0
25-34	168	30.9	49.9	19.2	100.0
35-44	127	37.0	52.2	10.8	100.0
45-54	135	31.2	50.4	18.4	100.0
55-64	79	17.1	48.8	34.1	100.0
65 and over	41	3.3	44.0	52.7	100.0

SOURCE: Data are from the follow-up survey of FSB recipients.

NOTE: Initial UI claim filed usually in late 1974 or early 1975. Distribution may not add to total because of rounding.

November 1977.[7] Table III.5 summarizes a few characteristics of those spells. Overall, the mean length of unemployment spells was about 61 weeks and that average was fairly uniform across most age-sex categories. Only

7. Only individuals who completed their initial unemployment spell prior to the second interview were considered in this analysis. Three percent of the sample was unemployed continuously from the UI claim date until the interview, and they were not included in the analysis.

TABLE III.5

Characteristics of the First Completed Unemployment Spell of FSB Recipients Starting at the Initial UI Claim Date[a], by Age and Sex

		Characteristic of Spell		
			Reason for End of Spell (Percentage of Recipients)	
Sex and Age	Sample Size	Mean Length of Completed Spell (Weeks)	Employment	Labor Force Withdrawal
All FSB Recipients	1,362	61.3	73.4%	26.6%
MALE				
Total	692	58.0	80.8	19.2
Under 25	191	48.0	92.7	7.3
25-34	163	52.2	90.8	9.2
35-44	95	65.6	92.6	7.4
45-54	90	65.3	86.7	13.3
55-64	90	70.5	58.9	41.1
65 and over	63	61.2	23.8	76.2
FEMALE				
Total	670	64.8	65.8	34.2
Under 25	115	58.6	76.5	23.5
25-34	164	67.3	68.3	31.7
35-44	121	70.0	83.5	16.5
45-54	136	67.1	70.6	29.4
55-64	89	59.7	41.6	58.4
65 and over	43	59.6	11.6	88.4

SOURCE: Data are from the follow-up survey of FSB recipients.

a. Usually in late 1974 or early 1975.

younger males had a mean duration of less than one year, and no group had a mean duration of over 71 weeks. Although it is not reflected in the table, the distribution of the length of unemployment spells was highly skewed. Over 17.5 percent of the sample had spells that lasted more than 100 weeks. The standard deviation for the entire sample was 45 weeks. Given the sample sizes, this variability makes most of the differences in cell means reported in table III.5 statistically insignificant. Only for young males is there significant evidence of shorter completed unemployment spells.

The initial unemployment spells of FSB recipients could have ended in one of two ways: reemployment or labor market withdrawal. The lower portion of table III.5 shows the proportions of respondents by those reasons, and by age and sex. Nearly three-quarters of all initial unemployment ended in reemployment. For males there was a clear correlation between increasing withdrawal from the labor force and increasing age. More than three-quarters of male FSB recipients age 65 and over ended their unemployment spell by leaving the labor force. Females exhibited a generally similar pattern, but there was significantly more labor force withdrawal in the 25- to 34-year-old age category compared with adjacent age categories. Child-care responsibilities may explain this pattern.

Labor Market Activities in November 1977

By the time the November 1977 interview was given— approximately three years after the initial layoff—57 percent of the recipients were employed (see table III.6), and that figure represented a substantial increase over the 31 percent employment rate recorded at the first interview (March 1976). Nevertheless, large numbers of FSB recipients remained unemployed. The implied unemployment rate[8] for the sample was nearly 23 percent (compared with over 60 percent in March 1976). More than 26 percent of the sample was out of the labor force in November 1977, which represents a 5 percentage point increase from the figure recorded on the initial interview.

---

8. This is the percentage of the sample that was unemployed, divided by the percentage that was in the labor force (i.e., the percentage that was either employed or unemployed).

TABLE III.6

Percentage Distribution of FSB Recipients, by Labor Force Status in November 1977, by Age and Sex

Sex and Age	Sample Size	Labor Force Status			
		Employed	Unemployed	Out Of Labor Force	Total
TOTAL	1,516	57.0%	16.7%	26.3%	100.0%
MALE					
Total	766	62.9	17.9	19.2	100.0
Under 25	193	79.8	16.6	3.6	100.0
25-34	174	79.3	16.1	4.6	100.0
35-44	106	74.5	22.6	2.8	100.0
45-54	102	56.9	24.5	18.6	100.0
55-64	110	39.1	15.5	45.5	100.0
65 and over	81	12.3	13.6	74.1	100.0
FEMALE					
Total	750	51.1	15.6	33.4	100.0
Under 25	119	58.8	12.6	28.6	100.0
25-34	185	58.9	15.1	25.9	100.0
35-44	134	64.9	23.1	11.9	100.0
45-54	149	55.7	15.4	28.9	100.0
55-64	103	27.2	13.6	59.2	100.0
65 and over	60	10.0	8.3	81.7	100.0

SOURCE: Data are from the follow-up survey of FSB recipients.

NOTE: Distribution may not add to total because of rounding.

Age and sex were important determinants of labor market status. Males were significantly more likely to be reemployed than females, and, particularly among males, younger individuals were more likely to be reemployed than older ones. These differences in employment rates were reflected in implied unemployment rates that ranged from less than 17 percent for young males to more than 50 percent for males in the 65-and-over category. Labor force participation rates also mirrored the employment pattern, ranging from a high of over 96 percent for young males to less than 19 percent for older females. Over 62 percent of all FSB recipients age 55 and over were out of the labor force in November 1977. Our analysis indicated that the vast majority of these individuals probably retired.

As reported above, 57 percent of the FSB sample was employed at the November 1977 interview date. It is interesting to compare the jobs held at that date with the jobs respondents held prior to the start of their UI spell (what we call their "pre-UI" jobs). Such a comparison provides an indication of the relative attractiveness of jobs held by the respondents and how successful they were in making a long term adjustment to their original job loss.

Analysis of this question indicated that there was a significant decline in the percentage employed in manufacturing—from nearly 50 percent on the pre-UI job to less than 40 percent at the interview date. This result mirrored the general failure of manufacturing employment to return to its nationwide pre-recession level. However, the drop in our sample was far more severe than the national data indicate. The large decrease in manufacturing employment was matched by an almost identical increase in service employment, a result that reflected national trends.

About one quarter of the respondents were back in their pre-UI jobs at the date of the second interview. This result, however, depended significantly on the industry in which those jobs were. Individuals who worked at a pre-UI job in durables manufacturing were more than twice as likely to get that job back than were individuals in other industries. Individuals working in durables manufacturing constituted nearly half (47 percent) of all respondents who did return to their previous employment. This result is consistent with other research findings that indicate layoffs subject to recall are more prevalent in durable goods manufacturing than in other industries. Our result shows not only the quantitative importance of this phenomenon, but, also, that at least during the mid 1970s recession, the duration of layoffs in durables manufacturing was, for some workers, far longer than the typical "temporary" layoff.

Table III.7 compares weekly earnings and hours of employed FSB recipients on their new (current) jobs as of November 1977, with their pre-UI jobs. To allow for general increases in wage levels since the end of the pre-UI job, earnings reported on that job were inflated by the percentage increase in average weekly nonagricultural wages over the period. In terms of 1977 dollars, average weekly earnings were about 10 percent lower on respondents' current jobs than on their pre-UI jobs. Slightly more than half that decline is attributed to a reduction in average hours worked per week, and the remainder is accounted for by a $.17 decline in average hourly earnings (from $5.01 to $4.84). Respondents over 55 years old experienced the largest reduction, both in hours and earnings. Younger individuals (under age 25) actually experienced increases in weekly earnings. For younger males there was also a slight increase in hours worked.

These data, therefore, give the impression that respondents' current jobs were somewhat less remunerative than their pre-UI jobs but that these differences were slight, at least for individuals in "prime" age working categories. However, this summary picture is misleading. Examination of data (not reported in the table) on the distribution of earnings changes experienced by individuals show that fewer than half the respondents had current weekly earnings that were within 25 percent of their (inflated) pre-UI earnings. Nearly one-third of the sample had current jobs that paid less than

TABLE III.7

Comparison of Hours and Earnings on Current Job (as of November 1977) to Pre-UI Job[a] for FSB Recipients, by Age and Sex

		Job Measure				
		Weekly Earnings (dollars)			Hours per Week	
Sex and Age	Sample Size	Current Job	Pre-UI Job	Pre-UI Job (1977 dollars)	Current Job	Pre-UI Job
TOTAL	836	$184	$167	$202	38.0	40.3
MALE						
Total	461	230	206	250	40.9	42.1
Under 25	150	197	158	191	41.4	40.9
25-34	129	251	223	270	42.2	42.6
35-44	75	278	232	282	41.9	43.5
45-54	55	243	249	302	40.9	43.2
55-64	41	218	221	270	37.5	42.9
65 and over	11	75	202	251	25.0	33.2
FEMALE						
Total	375	128	121	146	34.7	38.1
Under 25	66	143	109	130	35.9	36.9
25-34	106	130	121	147	35.6	38.5
35-44	88	136	129	156	35.9	38.9
45-54	82	111	111	136	32.7	37.2
55-64	28	126	115	141	33.7	39.4
65 and over	5	30	114	145	9.0	39.0

SOURCE: Data are from the initial and following FSB surveys.

a. Pre-UI job ended usually in late 1974 or early 1975.

75 percent of the pay level of their pre-UI jobs. That reduction was experienced by a significant number of prime age workers and it was not only attributable to the reduced hours noted for the older workers in the sample. Hence, even among those FSB recipients who had found jobs by the interview date, substantial numbers continued to face problems posed by their job loss and long unemployment spell. Of course, some workers managed to improve significantly on their pre-UI earnings. About 22 percent of all employed

respondents had current earnings at least 25 percent above those of their pre-UI jobs. Men and women were equally likely to experience such large increases. There is some indication that these increases were more prevalent among younger workers.

D. Conclusion

The brief description of FSB recipients presented in this chapter leads to two general conclusions regarding their characteristics. First, FSB recipients were more likely to be women and more likely to be older than other groups that were unemployed during the recession of the mid 1970s. This result stems partly from lower UI eligibility rates among younger workers and may also have been the result of weaker alternative economic opportunities for women and older workers. Second, FSB recipients had, in general, a long record of employment—having worked an average of 17 years, including 5 years at the job held prior to receiving UI benefits. Wages earned in these pre-UI jobs averaged slightly lower than the national average for production and nonsupervisory workers within the same industries.

Following the layoff that led eventually to FSB, recipients were unemployed for a substantial length of time—an average of 61 weeks during their initial completed spell. Three-quarters of these unemployment spells ended in reemployment and the remainder with withdrawal from the labor force. For males, increasing age was correlated with withdrawal from the labor force. By the time of the second interview, approximately three years after the initial layoff, 57 percent of FSB recipients were employed, with males and younger individuals having had relatively greater success finding work. Unemployment rates for all groups were high, however. Compared with pre-UI jobs, the nature of jobs held by reemployed recipients at the second interview was extremely varied. Nearly one-third of all reemployed individuals experienced a reduction in real weekly wages of 25 percent or more, and the average weekly wage fell by about 10 percent. Declines in weekly wages were about equally affected by decreases in hours worked and by decreases in hourly wage rates.

IV. ALLOCATIONAL EFFECTS OF FSB

A. Introduction

This chapter evaluates the FSB program from the perspective of economic efficiency. That is, it examines ways in which FSB affected the overall allocation of economic resources. Five additional sections follow. Section B develops a general rationale, based on microeconomic considerations, for extension of UI benefits during recessions. Issues basic to evaluating any extended benefits program are discussed. Section C examines these issues in the FSB context. Section D shifts to macroeconomic concerns and describes how extended UI benefits may help achieve stabilization goals. The actual performance of FSB in that regard is examined in section E. Finally, section F provides an overall assessment of FSB's allocational impact.

B. Microeconomic Issues in UI Benefit Extensions

One way to analyze the allocational impact of UI benefit extensions is to consider them as "insurance" which provides workers some degree of earnings protection in the event of layoff. As with any insurance policy, its protection is valuable because it reduces financial risks. In the absence of a government program, it is probable that workers would seek such protection for themselves.[1] Most insurance poses

1. An example of this would be a worker who chooses job stability over high wages.

the problem of "moral hazard"—that is, being insured increases the probability of incurring the risk (here, unemployment). Because unemployment insurance reduces the cost of being unemployed, it encourages individuals to be more selective about the jobs they are willing to accept or to reduce the intensity of their job search, and thereby prolongs their unemployment. What labor economists term "work disincentives" and what insurance economists term "moral hazard" amount to the same thing in the case of unemployment insurance.

Present UI provisions—specifically partial wage replacement, limited benefit duration, the waiting week, and availability-for-work and job search requirements—reflect society's preference concerning the trade-off between the program's beneficial earnings replacement effects and its negative work disincentives effects. Each of these factors prevents the existing UI system from providing complete insurance against wage loss to unemployed workers and can be viewed as an attempt to control "moral hazard." An insurance-based rationale for extending the potential duration of UI benefits during recessionary periods can be developed by examining how the trade-off between risk aversion and moral hazard changes during such periods.

Recessions obviously increase the risk of unemployment. This is partly due to an increased probability of being laid off and partly because of increased unemployment duration once a worker has been displaced. The second factor provides the impetus for benefit extensions. In their absence, recessions would increase the likelihood that UI recipients would remain unemployed sufficiently long to exhaust their benefit entitlements. In order to provide a degree of insurance protection similar to that of normal UI (i.e., enough to cover most periods of joblessness), it would be necessary to increase potential benefits durations. If the work disincentives resulting from such extensions were small, policy makers might choose to provide nearly complete insurance compensation. But if such disincentives were substantial, a policy of less than complete compensation might be preferable.[2]

A similar conclusion can be reached by means of job search theory, under which payment of UI may be viewed as efficient because it permits workers to hold out for better job matches. UI thereby improves the overall allocation of labor resources. Under this rationale, regular duration provisions reflect society's view of the point at which further efficiency gains from subsidized job search cease. Because the prevalence of job offers declines during recessions, it may be desirable to extend the period of subsidized search because this would presumably permit recipients to obtain better jobs than those they otherwise would be forced to accept. This job search perspective provides a less clear-cut prescription than does the insurance perspective about exactly how long extensions should be, but it does focus attention on post-employment wages—a topic that is typically neglected under the backward-looking insurance perspective.

Together, the insurance and job search efficiency arguments for extending UI benefits during recessions suggest three major empirical issues:

(1) To what extent do extended benefits programs compensate for lengthening unemployment durations brought on by recessions?

(2) Do such programs prompt individuals to stay unemployed longer?

2. This "optimal insurance" approach to UI benefit extensions is discussed in more detail in Nicholson and Corson (1980).

(3) To the extent job search is prolonged by receipt of extended benefits, does that longer search result in recipients' finding better jobs than those they would otherwise be forced to accept?

This paper examines each of these questions in the context of the FSB program. Because the issue of how well FSB compensated for lengthening unemployment spells has implications for assessing the distributional as well as the allocational consequences of the program, we will postpone a discussion of it until chapter V. In the next section we examine the other two issues.

C. Labor Market Effects of FSB

This section examines the effects of FSB on the labor market behavior of individuals. It is divided into two parts that reflect the empirical issues raised in the previous section: a discussion of the possible work disincentive effects of FSB, and an analysis of the effect of FSB on subsequent wage rates.

Effects of FSB on the Length of Unemployment Spells

There is by now a rather substantial research literature on the effects of unemployment insurance benefits on lengths of unemployment spells. Most of that literature focuses on the UI "wage replacement ratio" (that is, the ratio of UI benefits to net potential wages) and attempts to estimate the extent to which high values for that ratio lead to longer unemployment. Hamermesh (1977) concludes his summary of a number of studies with his "best" estimate that every 10 percentage point increase in the wage replacement ratio is associated with about one half week of additional unemployment. He also indicates a belief that the disincentive effects of UI are somewhat smaller than this during periods of labor market weakness, but the empirical support he offers for that proposition is weak.

How relevant the findings of overall work disincentives associated with UI wage replacement ratios are to the FSB program is unclear. If UI incorporates disincentives, extending the duration of potential benefits must in some way increase these. But because extended benefits programs (including FSB) have no effect on the weekly wage replacement ratio, there is no direct way to estimate the size of such effects from most of the empirical work.[3] A few studies have attempted to estimate directly the effects of different UI potential durations on the length of unemployment spells. Results for seven of these studies are summarized in table IV.1. For ease of comparison, all results are reported as the estimated impact of one additional week of potential duration on the length of an individual's unemployment spell, although not all of the studies cited actually stated their conclusions in that way. Overall, the impression given by table IV.1 is that results are extremely varied. Estimates range from insignificant effects (Ehrenberg-Oaxaca) to point estimates that imply that each week of potential duration leads to almost one week of unemployment (Holen and Walsh).

One way to narrow this range is to eliminate from consideration those studies that are based on problematic data.

3. If potential wages UI recipients can expect to receive decline with the duration of their unemployment, then individuals collecting FSB may have higher wage replacement ratios than otherwise similar individuals whose unemployment spells are just beginning. But this issue should more appropriately be considered in relation to the question of how wage replacement ratios are measured rather than to some direct FSB effect. Although various measures could be developed depending on how unemployed workers' "potential" wage is defined, we will continue common practice and identify the previous wage as the potential wage.

TABLE IV.1

Summary of Research on Disincentive Effects of Longer UI Potential Durations

Author[a]	Data Set	Effect of One Additional Week of Potential Duration on Length of Unemployment Spell	Comments
Ehrenberg-Oaxaca (1976)	National Longitudinal Survey (various age/sex groups)	0	Potential duration poorly measured—effect biased toward zero
Holen (1977)	UI recipients in five cities	0.8	Used compensated weeks as dependent variable—effect positively biased
Brewster et al. (1978)	FSB recipients in fifteen states	0.4-0.6	Simple use of potential duration as independent variable. Complete spell measured. Potential duration from administrative records
Walsh (1978)	Recipients of Redundancy Payments in Ireland	0.4-1.0	Larger estimated effect for weeks employed
Newton-Rosen (1979)	UI recipients in Georgia	0.4-0.5	Used weeks compensated and maximum likelihood procedure to reduce bias
Solon (1979)	UI exhaustees in New York	0.3[b]	Unusual independent variable used in place of potential duration—makes interpretation different
Moffitt-Nicholson (1979)	FSB recipients in fifteen states	0.1	Used kinked budget constraint and maximum likelihood procedure. Estimate based on weeks employed

a. For detailed references see Bibliography

b. Based on Solon's estimate that EB availability for 13 weeks increased unemployed weeks by 4. Solon estimate for the effect of EB availability on employment by "repeaters" (that is individuals who file for benefits in two or more successive years) was similar to this estimate also.

In particular, studies in which potential UI durations are poorly measured might be excluded because coefficients estimated for such variables will be biased toward zero (this is probably the case for the Ehrenberg-Oaxaca study). Similarly, studies that use weeks of UI received as a dependent variable will incorporate biases into their estimates because such a variable does not measure the full unemployment spell and is related to the way that potential UI durations are specified in state law. Only those studies based on weeks of compensation that take these problems explicitly into account should be considered.

Under these conditions, the Brewster et al., Newton-Rosen and Moffitt-Nicholson studies provide the most reliable estimates. According to these, each week of potential UI benefits increases the unemployment spell length by between 0.1 and 0.4 weeks. Some portion of the remaining disparities in these estimates arises from the fact that the smaller (Moffitt-Nicholson) estimate does not include the effect that additional weeks of benefits may have on inducing UI recipients to stay in the labor force rather than ceasing their job search efforts (because their study was limited only to labor market participants) whereas the larger estimates do, at least partly, include such effects. For the FSB program as a whole, then, the conclusion would be that the increase in average potential duration of about 24 weeks increased the length of unemployment spells by between 2.4 and 9.6 weeks where the larger of these figures also includes induced participation effects.

Independent estimates of the effect of extended benefits programs based on macroeconomic data are generally unavailable. It has not been possible to differentiate between the effects of such programs and of other economic factors on the lengths of unemployment spells. In one study of aggregate exhaustion rates, Nicholson and Corson (1978) found that availability of EB and FSB benefits did increase such rates. That finding provides implicit support for the notion that those programs also increased the length of unemployment spells. The quantitative size of such effects was roughly consistent with the smaller of the estimates from the microeconomic studies.

The overall conclusion then is that the FSB program did increase the average length of unemployment spell experienced by UI recipients by at least two and one-half weeks and perhaps significantly more if participation effects are taken into account. When applied to the 10.4 million individuals who collected a first UI payment in 1975, the 2.5 weeks figure implies there were about 26 million more weeks of unemployment that year than there would have been in the absence of FSB. In other words, about 6 percent of the total number of weeks of unemployment experienced by the civilian labor force in 1975 was attributable to FSB. Without FSB the overall unemployment rate that year would have been 7.9 percent instead of the 8.5 percent officially recorded. Allowing for participation effects would significantly increase this estimated discrepancy between the actual and potential unemployment rates.

FSB and Job Search

Work disincentive effects arising from receipt of UI benefits may be counterbalanced by beneficial job search outcomes. Continued availability of benefits permits individuals to hold out for, and perhaps ultimately to receive, higher wages. Hence, from an overall allocational perspective, the effect of UI is ambiguous—its negative work disincentive must be weighed against its positive promotion of better job matches. Which effect dominates remains an unanswered, empirical question. Some authors (Ehrenberg and Oaxaca, 1976 and Holen, 1977) have reported both significant disincentive effects and significant positive subsequent wage effects. Classen (1977), however, found only significant disincentive effects with no observable wage effects. These widely differing results may be explained by the absence of any universally agreed-upon conceptual model of the job search process and by the different statistical methodologies employed by the authors. An indirect test of the beneficial job search impact of UI benefits is provided by the literature on reservation wages and search intensity. Despite a strong theoretical presumption that UI benefit levels should affect reservation wages, there is practically no empirical support for the proposition (see Crosslin, 1975). Similarly, the effect of UI on search intensity has been found to be positive in some studies (Crosslin, 1975) and negative in others (Barron and Mellow, 1979). All of these studies are subject to methodological criticisms, and in any case, the precise connection between search strategies and ultimate wages has not been clearly documented.

Given the paucity of research on job search effects of regular UI and the contradictory findings of the few existing studies, it is not surprising that there is virtually no literature on the job search effects of FSB-type extended benefits programs. In theory, the direction of such effects seems clear enough. Extended benefits programs raise the extent to which UI compensates individuals for their unemployment spells (although the programs do not change the wage replacement ratio occurring during periods of benefit collection) and that should induce individuals to adopt higher reservation wages. This in turn should cause recipients to extend the duration of their unemployment spells and to hold out for ultimately higher wage rates. The first effect has already been described in the previous section where it was shown that increases in potential UI durations do seem to lead to increases in observed unemployment durations. Whether this increased unemployment is used productively to search for better jobs is the issue here.

Empirical evidence on the effect of extended UI durations on job search productivity is extremely meager. Among those studies of regular UI recipients that attempt to estimate the wage effect of changes in potential duration, only the Holen (1977) paper reports a significant impact. Her estimate suggests that each week of additional potential duration results in a $2.50 increase in post-unemployment quarterly earnings—presumably attributed to the prolonged and more effective job search made possible by the added duration. But, as Holen herself points out, this estimate may be biased upward by the relationship between individuals' prior weeks of employment and their regular UI duration eligibility since prior weeks of employment are also correlated with future earnings.

Only the Corson et al. (1977) and Brewster et al. (1978) studies of FSB recipients explicitly considered the effects of longer potential duration on job search among extended benefits recipients. Those studies found little in the way of significant effects. Regardless of whether job search activities were measured in terms of results (i.e., post-unemployment wage) or in terms of inputs to the search process (i.e., reservation wages or various measures of search intensity), no consistent effects of longer potential duration were found. But because these studies were limited to the relatively long term unemployed, the results do not really answer the question of how variations in UI potential durations might affect a more representative group of recipients.

In conclusion, very little is known about how changes in potential durations affect recipients' job search. On the theoretical level there is some presumption that increases in potential duration should lead to better job matches for approximately the same reasons that changes in UI benefit levels might. But empirical support for that proposition is virtually nonexistent. The issue remains open.

D. Macroeconomic Issues in UI Benefit Extensions

In addition to affecting individual UI recipients' decisions, extensions in potential duration also have effects on the overall economic activity level. The general theory behind these "macroeconomic" effects is described in this section, followed in the next section by some empirical evidence about the actual performance of FSB in that regard.

One purpose of UI benefits is to cushion the decline in disposable income that occurs during a recession and thereby to stabilize the overall level of aggregate demand and macroeconomic activity. For regular UI benefits, this result is more or less "automatic." No discretionary policy decision is necessary because the regular program simply absorbs a larger caseload and pays out higher aggregate levels of benefits as layoffs increase during the early stages of a downturn. In this respect, the automatic stabilization provided by regular UI benefits is similar to that provided by the automatic reduction in federal tax receipts during recessions, although of a much smaller dollar magnitude.[4] For the extended benefits (EB) program, the argument is similar but more complicated. Since 1970, EB benefits have been "triggered" automatically as national or state insured unemployment rates increase. Frequently, these trigger requirements

4. For example, VonFurstenberg (1976) found that differences between actual and "full employment" UI benefits (regular plus EB) were less than 22 percent of the decline (below full employment levels) in federal tax revenues during each of the recession years since 1958. Similar results are suggested by the data in table IV.2, described below.

have been modified in response to recessionary indicators (for example, rising exhaustion rates). Hence, although they are not so "automatic" as regular UI benefits or federal tax collections, EB benefits can, for most purposes, be so categorized along with the regular programs. Those benefits represented about 23 percent of total regular UI benefits during the recession of the mid 1970s.

Contrary to the automatic character of the regular UI and EB programs, FSB-type programs are usually regarded as "discretionary," that is, the programs have been implemented through explicit legislative action in response to a perceived policy need. From a stabilization perspective, therefore, it is appropriate to compare FSB to other discretionary fiscal policies. In making that comparison on a theoretical level, two criteria are of central concern: the size of the "multipliers" and the relative flexibility with which FSB can be implemented in response to stabilization needs.[5] With respect to the first issue, there is general agreement that the multiplier for government transfer payments (such as FSB) is fairly large. It is clearly larger than the multiplier for tax reductions (because transfer recipients spend a higher fraction of their incomes than do taxpayers in general) and it may be nearly as large as the multiplier for government expenditures on goods and services. Whether there are reasons to expect the multiplier for extended UI benefits to differ at all from the one for other government transfer programs is unclear. On the one hand, UI recipients may have higher incomes than do other transfer recipients, thereby implying a somewhat smaller multiplier. On the other hand, because UI benefits are more closely related to temporary declines in family income than are other transfer payments, there is

5. A third issue, the macroeconomic effect of financing FSB or other discretionary fiscal policy, will not be discussed here because, to a first approximation, FSB would be a little different from other policies.

probably a high marginal propensity to spend out of such income to maintain existing living standards, and hence the multiplier would be correspondingly high. There is no clear way to differentiate between these theoretical probabilities, and empirical research on the matter is virtually nonexistent.

With respect to legislative and administrative flexibility, FSB-type emergency benefit extensions have a number of advantages. Because the programs operate through an existing administrative mechanism, payments can be initiated quickly without developing a new payments process. Of course, recessionary tax rate reductions share the same advantage, but withholding procedures and filing dates do constrain their flexibility to some degree. UI extensions can also be more quickly implemented than either federal spending or federal employment programs because much less planning and attention to the nature of individual projects is required. Finally, though more conjecturally, UI extensions provide a more flexible policy response to recessions because the political intricacies involved in implementing them may be less complex than for most other spending policies.

Of course, extending UI benefits is not a perfectly flexible fiscal policy. There may be lags in implementation arising from the need to coordinate federal policies with existing state UI systems, and peak-load problems in local offices may inhibit the timely disbursement of payments. Phasing out extended benefits programs also involves some inflexibility—primarily because of the built-in inertia which provides recipients with a relatively large number of additional weeks of eligibility (two 13-week segments in the case of FSB, for example). On the whole, however, these inflexibilities are probably of minor importance compared with other discretionary fiscal policies.

From a theoretical perspective, FSB-type emergency extensions compare rather favorably to other macrostabilization policies. They have both the flexibility and the potential multiplier impact on aggregate demand to warrant consideration as an important policy option. Of course, such a conclusion is based on *a priori* considerations and does not address the actual performance of FSB—a subject to which we now turn.

E. Macroeconomic Performance of FSB

In this section we will examine two aspects of the actual macroeconomic performance of FSB: (1) the importance of FSB relative to other federal stabilization measures during the recession of the mid 1970s and, (2) administrative and technical problems involved in implementing and phasing out FSB. Information on the first of these questions is presented in table IV.2 which shows total FSB benefits paid during the 1974-77 period. For comparison purposes, table IV.2 also presents data for the same period on total UI benefits, on the federal budget deficit, and on two other discretionary fiscal policies: outlays for public service employment and discretionary tax rate reductions.[6] Three general conclusions may be drawn from these data. First, during the 1974-75 recession, FSB benefits constituted a relatively small portion of all discretionary fiscal policies. Payments under the program accounted for less than 10 percent of the "full employment" deficit and, of course, made up an even smaller fraction of the actual federal deficit. Tax reduction (both automatic and legislated) clearly played a far more important role in both automatic and discretionary federal stabilization efforts.

6. The table provides data on both the actual federal budget deficit and the "full employment" deficit. The latter concept adjusts the actual deficit for the effect of the business cycle itself on the expenditures and tax collections and is therefore a better measure of discretionary fiscal policy.

TABLE IV.2

Comparison of UI, FSB and Other Federal Stabilization Policies, 1974-77 (Quarterly Data are Annualized in $Billions)

Calendar Quarter	Federal Deficit Actual	Federal Deficit Full Employment Estimate[a]	All UI Payments[b]	FSB Payments	Public Service Employment Expenditures	Tax Cuts[c]
1974.1	5.5	1.3	5.4	--	0.5	--
.2	7.6	3.5	6.3	--	0.2	--
.3	8.0	4.5	7.3	--	0.3	--
.4	21.7	2.5	9.4	--	0.4	--
1975.1	48.0	6.9	15.1	0.8	1.1	1.8
.2	99.9	55.2	18.6	1.8	2.7	42.3
.3	66.3	29.9	18.7	2.5	2.0	15.2
.4	68.2	32.3	17.6	3.5	2.5	15.0
1976.1	57.5	28.6	17.7	3.8	2.7	12.9
.2	47.3	21.0	15.3	3.3	2.8	12.8
.3	52.2	27.0	14.7	2.1	2.4	11.6
.4	57.4	30.9	14.7	2.0	2.8	11.8
1977.1	37.2	26.5	15.1	2.1	2.4	1.4
.2	40.9	27.7	12.3	1.5	2.9	3.4
.3	53.6	40.2	11.6	0.9	3.7	7.9
.4	53.6	42.2	11.8	0.5	4.9	6.7

SOURCE: *Survey of Current Business.* Annual Surveys of Fiscal Policy.

a. Based on estimated budget outlays and revenues assuming unemployment rate of 5 percent "full employment" level.

b. Includes UI, EB, FSB and SUA (Special Unemployment Assistance, a temporary program that paid benefits during the period to workers not yet covered by UI).

c. For 1975-76 includes the Tax Reduction Act of 1975, the Revenue Adjustment Act of 1975, and the Tax Reform Act for 1976. For 1977 includes only the Tax Reduction and Simplification Act of 1977. Reductions estimated assuming full employment.

Second, the data in table IV.2 show that even though FSB benefits were small relative to the overall federal budget, they were relatively large when compared with all UI benefits or with spending under public service employment programs. During the period 1975.3-1976.2 (when FSB benefits for a full 26-week period were in effect in practically all states), payments under FSB amounted to about 20 percent of all UI benefits and to perhaps as much as 30 percent of "recession induced" (those being paid because of the above normal levels of unemployment) UI benefits. Hence, FSB contributed in a major way to the stabilizing ability of the UI system as a whole. Similarly, for most of the quarters during the recession, FSB benefits totaled more than expenditures under public service employment programs, so they shouldn't be regarded as trivial to overall stabilization efforts.

A third conclusion is that the actual timing of FSB benefit payments during the 1975-76 period was not precisely consistent with the needs of stabilization policy. Aggregate payments did not peak until 1976.1, a period well after the trough of the recession had been passed. Similarly, FSB benefit levels in the first two quarters of 1975 were relatively small although these were probably the quarters during which the benefits were most needed for maintaining aggregate purchasing power. The reason for this lag in the growth of FSB benefits relates to the particular way in which FSB was implemented and to the nature of its relationship with the regular UI program. We now examine these issues.

A first obvious reason for the lag in the start of large-scale spending under FSB is simply that it took time for individuals suffering layoffs in the early stages of the recession (say, November or December 1974) to be unemployed long enough to qualify for FSB. Regular UI plus EB provided individuals with 1.5 times their regular UI entitlement, which for many recipients (though not, of course, for all workers) amounted to 39 weeks of benefits. Hence, the majority of workers laid off in late 1974 might have started to collect FSB sometime in the third quarter of 1975. The sharp upswing in FSB benefits in 1975.3 and 1975.4 reflects exactly this lagged response to the recessionary layoffs.[7] Benefit payments during early 1975, on the other hand, went primarily to individuals who had been laid off prior to the recession but had not ended their UI benefit years when FSB went into effect. These individuals constituted a "backlog" that became eligible for benefits immediately upon implementation of the FSB program.[8] The presence of this lag between recessionary layoffs and the actual buildup of FSB payments makes it necessary to modify somewhat the theoretical notion that emergency UI extensions represent highly flexible and responsive tools for macroeconomic stabilization purposes. Rather, the lag between policy implementation and the ultimate timing of its impact should be clearly recognized.

Although purely administrative implementation problems also caused some part of the lag in the buildup of FSB benefit payments, the effect was probably negligible. By the end of the first quarter of 1975 all states had reached agreement with the Department of Labor to begin paying benefits, and operational problems in making those payments were relatively small despite the peak load problems being experienced by local UI offices. Probably more significant

7. The increase in caseloads also reflected implementation of the second tier of FSB in March 1975.

8. Because of the way in which UI benefit years are defined, some individuals in the FSB backlog had lost their jobs well before 1974. The Mathematica sample of FSB recipients contains a small number of individuals who started a benefit year as early as 1971, for example. This occurred because some individuals had exhausted their EB entitlement but had not found subsequent reemployment in states that had not gone off EB since 1971 (primarily Washington). For these individuals, FSB represented a pure windfall.

from a macroeconomic perspective were the legislative and operational difficulties involved in finally terminating the FSB program. As table IV.2 shows, FSB benefits continued at an annual rate of over $2.0 billion into the first quarter of 1977, more than a year and one-half after the low point of economic activity. This occurred because FSB was gradually phased out state-by-state via trigger mechanisms and because, even when new claims were no longer being accepted under FSB, individuals already collecting benefits were entitled to their full extensions. Of course, it might be argued that fiscal stimulation was still needed for the economy well into 1977, but whether FSB was an appropriate policy for that purpose remains an open issue. On the one hand, FSB benefits, because they were concentrated in areas of high unemployment, probably did continue to exert a beneficial effect on local economies. On the other hand, from a macroeconomic perspective, it may be the case that stimulative policies in the upswing of the business cycle are better focused on investment than on consumption activities and therefore other policies might have dominated FSB in long term effectiveness.

F. Conclusion

In this chapter we have developed conceptual bases for judging the allocational effects of emergency extended UI benefits programs and have reviewed some FSB program impacts on these effects. For some issues, the FSB-provided evidence seems relatively clear. For example, although there is some uncertainty about the precise size of the effect, there seems to be sufficient empirical support for the proposition that longer potential UI durations do provide an incentive for individuals to remain unemployed longer. On a macroeconomic level, FSB benefits were shown to have potentially stabilizing effects, although the program did exhibit some shortcomings in terms of the precise timing of its fiscal impact. Relative to discretionary tax reductions and various automatic stabilizers, however, the effect of FSB was quite small.

Although the analysis of FSB so far does clarify some allocational questions, several others remain relatively untouched. There is, for example, no very good evidence about the effect of FSB benefits on recipients' job search behavior. Nor has there been an empirical investigation of how the macroeconomic effects of FSB might differ from the effects of other federal transfer programs. Answers to these and several other questions are needed if we are to have a complete assessment of the allocational effects of emergency UI extensions.

V. DISTRIBUTIONAL EFFECTS OF FSB

A. Introduction

In this chapter we examine two distributional arguments for extension of FSB during recessions. The first, which we term the "intertemporal equity argument," concerns the question of whether workers laid off during recessions are treated by UI in a way similar to workers laid off during normal periods, and the extent to which extensions are necessary to assure similarity of treatment. A second argument for extensions—what we call the "income maintenance argument"—concerns the necessity of providing extended benefits to low income workers during recessions. Our examination of these arguments begins in section B with a brief analysis of the intertemporal equity issue and is followed in section C with a more extended treatment of the question for FSB specifically. Section D considers the theoretical income maintenance arguments for benefit extensions, followed by an analysis (in section E) of the FSB experience. Section F provides a brief summary of our analysis of distributional issues.

B. Intertemporal Equity and Benefit Extensions

One goal of the UI system is to provide insurance protection for individuals suffering a loss of earnings through involuntary unemployment. Because of financial constraints and potential disincentive effects, only a portion of lost weekly earnings is replaced by UI and the duration of benefits is limited. Consequently, it is necessary to develop a measure of "adequacy" in order to judge how well the UI system meets its protection goals. Most discussions of this concept have focused on the weekly benefit amount and compared it to both past earnings and to a recipient's "nondeferrable" or "recurrent" expenses. The assumption behind this latter concept is that if UI benefits cover recurrent expenses (food, mortgage payments, and so forth), individuals will not be forced to make major spending pattern adjustments while unemployed. Any loss in their standards of living will be limited and temporary; their standards will return to pre-layoff levels once they are reemployed. Clearly, the potential duration of benefits is an important factor in determining the adequacy of UI protection. If benefits covered only a small part of an individual's layoff period, they would be judged inadequate regardless of how high weekly payments were. Furthermore, potential durations that might be judged adequate during nonrecessionary periods might be inadequate during the lengthy unemployment spells of a recession. This latter point suggests a rationale for the extension of benefits during recessionary periods: if we wish to treat individuals equally in terms of benefit adequacy, those laid off during recessions should be eligible for longer potential durations of UI than individuals laid off during nonrecessionary periods. This argument is similar to the insurance rationale for extensions presented in the previous chapter, where it was shown that extensions may be required to maintain the "optimal" level of insurance protection when labor market conditions worsen. Both arguments suggest focusing on how well extended benefits programs compensate for the effects of lengthening unemployment during recessions. We now examine that question for FSB.

C. FSB Coverage of Lengthening Unemployment Spells During the 1974-75 Recession

In this section we examine the extent to which extended benefits provided under FSB compensated for the longer unemployment spells experienced by individuals. The discussion is divided into three parts. The first part examines some general measures of labor market experiences during the 1974-75 recession and describes the difficulties involved in using those measures to appraise FSB. Next, we examine UI exhaustion rates and the effect of FSB upon them. Finally, we show that exhaustion rates alone may not provide a complete picture of UI adequacy during recessions and propose a more general measure of the overall earnings replacement that UI provides.

Unemployment Spells During the Recession

It is clear that the average length of unemployment spells increased substantially during the recession of the mid 1970s. Table V.1 reports some general measures of unemployment during that period, including a summary of the unemployment spell figures customarily published from the Current Population Survey (CPS).[1] These data show that as the national total unemployment rate rose from 5 percent in the first quarter of 1974 to nearly 9 percent in 1975.2, the reported median length of unemployment spells rose from 4.7 weeks to nearly 9 weeks. Even more significant from the perspective of UI extended benefits programs, the proportion of all unemployment spells accounted for by spells that were currently over 26 weeks in duration rose dramatically from only 7 percent of the total in 1974.1 to more than 20

1. This survey is conducted monthly by the Census Bureau and is the principal source of U.S. labor market data.

TABLE V.1

Unemployment Measures During the Mid 1970s

Calendar Quarter	Total Unemployment Rate	Current Unemployment Spells[a] Average Duration (Weeks)	Median Duration (Weeks)	Percentage Over 26 Weeks	Insured Unemployment Rate[b]
1974.1	5.0	9.5	4.7	7.0	3.2
2	5.1	9.7	4.8	7.5	3.3
3	5.6	9.9	5.0	7.6	3.3
4	6.7	9.9	5.1	7.4	4.4
1975.1	8.2	11.3	6.9	9.3	5.8
2	8.9	13.9	8.8	13.6	6.5
3	8.5	15.5	9.0	18.4	6.1
4	8.3	16.2	9.1	19.8	5.3
1976.1	7.7	16.5	8.7	21.0	4.2
2	7.6	15.9	7.9	18.5	4.4
3	7.7	15.5	7.8	16.7	4.8
4	7.7	15.2	8.0	17.0	4.7
1977.1	7.5	14.8	7.4	16.5	4.0
2	7.2	14.6	6.9	15.2	3.8
3	6.9	13.9	7.1	13.8	4.0
4	6.6	13.6	6.9	13.4	3.9

SOURCES: Columns 1-4 *Employment and Earnings,* various issues. Column 5 *Unemployment Insurance Statistics,* various issues.
NOTE: All data are national figures, seasonally adjusted.
a. Spell duration represents continuous weeks of unemployment up to time of monthly survey.
b. Insured unemployment rates reflect regular UI claimants only. EB and FSB claimants are excluded.

percent of the larger totals in late 1975 and early 1976. This expansion in the incidence of long unemployment spells also had the effect of increasing the reported average spell length substantially.

Using these published figures on the length of unemployment spells to assess the desirability of the benefit extensions incorporated into the FSB program poses a number of difficulties. First, the data include many unemployed individuals who were not eligible for UI (new entrants and UI exhaustees, for example). Exactly how the length of completed unemployment spells of UI recipients changed during the recession is not known. Second, CPS data on unemployment spells are known to exhibit a number of conceptual problems that make it difficult to infer from them what is actually happening to individuals' unemployment spells.[2] And, third, UI and the CPS use different tests to differentiate between individuals who are temporarily unemployed and those who are out of the labor force. It is possible that many of the individuals identified as being long term unemployed in the CPS would not meet UI "availability for work" requirements. Also, the CPS data include UI exhaustees who cannot collect additional UI during their present unemployment spell. Hence, the CPS data may overstate the unemployment duration of UI recipients. These combined shortcomings of the CPS data make it impossible to ascertain the extent to which the incidence of relatively long unemployment spells increased among individuals eligible for UI during the recession of the mid 1970s.

2. See, for example, Kaitz (1970) who points out that there are two opposite biases in the CPS figures. The fact that the CPS does not measure completed spells but rather spells in progress biases estimated spell lengths downward. The fact that the CPS oversamples those with long spells biases estimated spell lengths upward. During periods when average spell lengths are increasing, this second effect is likely to become the more important bias.

About all that can be concluded from the CPS data on lengthy unemployment spells is that the prevalence of such spells obviously increased and that the intertemporal equity criterion suggests that UI benefits should have been extended to cover some portion of them. Whether extensions under EB alone would have been sufficient for that purpose is difficult to say. Data on mean and median spell lengths from the CPS suggest that EB was insufficient because these indicators increased by much more than the 50 percent expansion in UI entitlement that EB provides. But such calculations are, at best, only indicative of the need for an FSB-type emergency program and provide little guidance as to the shape such a program should take. To obtain more specific insights into the question requires the use of other indicators.

Effect of FSB on Exhaustion Rates

One indicator of the need for FSB-type extensions is provided by studies of UI exhaustion rates and how they were affected by FSB availability. Because FSB provided as many as 26 additional weeks of benefits, it presumably had a significant impact on the probability that any individual completely exhausted his or her full UI entitlement. Assessing the precise size of that effect is made difficult, however, by the absence of detailed longitudinal data for a random sample of UI recipients from which exhaustion rates might be measured directly. Rather, exhaustion rates under FSB must be inferred from existing program data, from various special samples of UI recipients, and from aggregate statistical studies. Here we review these sources of information and conclude that they show a reasonably consistent picture—that FSB reduced total exhaustion rates for UI during the recession of the mid 1970s to levels well below those that characterized regular UI during nonrecessionary periods.

Table V.2 presents quarterly aggregate program data on the number of first and final payments made to recipients under state UI programs and under FSB for the period 1973.1 to 1977.4. The table also shows the ratio of the number of UI final payments to the number of UI first payments, lagged two quarters, which, although it poses a number of difficult interpretational problems, is a figure frequently referred to as "the" exhaustion rate for regular UI.[3] Because quarterly exhaustion rates defined in this way have major seasonal components, five-quarter moving averages of the rates are reported in the table. These data show that immediately prior to the recession, about 30 percent of UI recipients were exhausting their regular UI benefits, a figure somewhat above the 25 percent norm usually believed to characterize the UI program during periods of relatively full employment. During the recession (roughly the period 1974.4-1975.4, a period long enough to include the lagged effects of the sharp downturn in late 1974), exhaustion rates for regular UI were about 10-12 percentage points above the pre-recession levels. That is, during the recession, approximately 40-42 percent of UI recipients exhausted their regular benefit entitlement.

Did FSB, in combination with the permanent standby EB program, succeed in substantially mitigating this recession-induced rise in regular UI exhaustion rates? Although the absence of detailed longitudinal data on regular UI recipients during the period precludes an exact answer, EB and FSB program data (reported in table V.3) provide a rough

3. As an approximation to the theoretical concept of the probability that an individual UI recipient will exhaust his or her benefits, this calculated exhaustion ratio is subject to biases arising from aggregation, seasonality, the changing composition of the pool of UI recipients (especially in states with variable duration provisions), and the complex effects that accompany changes in UI duration provisions. Aggregate data must be used, however, because theoretically correct exhaustion probabilities from program operating data are not available on a regular basis.

TABLE V.2

Quarterly Program Data for Regular UI and FSB, 1973-77

Calendar Quarter	Regular UI Program[a] First Payments (Thousands)	Final Payments (Thousands)	Moving Average Exhaustion Rate[b]	FSB Program[a] First Payments (Thousands)	Final Payments (Thousand)
1973.1	1791	422	0.28	--	--
2	1074	397	0.30	--	--
3	1256	342	0.30	--	--
4	1207	333	0.32	--	--
1974.1	2455	421	0.29	--	--
2	1304	504	0.33	--	--
3	1622	509	0.36	--	--
4	2348	492	0.40	--	--
1975.1	4064	737	0.38	435	40
2	2466	1210	0.41	597	266
3	2100	1255	0.43	755	430
4	1935	976	0.43	874	476
1976.1	2908	953	0.37	753	514
2	1705	864	0.39	667	434
3	1937	767	0.40	410	285
4	2036	701	0.38	388	267
1977.1	3040	811	0.35	428	267
2	1530	776	0.36	344	282
3	1732	667	0.36	297	158
4	1682	592	0.35	107	202

SOURCE: Regular Unemployment Insurance First and Final Payments from *Unemployment Insurance Statistics* (various issues). Exhaustion rates calculated by the author. FSB data from special tabulations provided by the Unemployment Insurance Service of the U.S. Department of Labor's Employment and Training Administration.

a. Excludes recipients who drew benefits under federal unemployment compensation programs for federal civil service employees (UCFE) and ex-military servicemen (UCX).

b. Five quarter moving averages of quarterly exhaustion rates calculated as final payments in each quarter divided by first payments in quarter ending six months earlier.

estimate of the effects. These data indicate that EB exhaustion rates during the 1974-1977 period averaged about 66 percent. Hence availability of EB alone reduced the exhaustion rate from about 40 percent for regular UI to about 26-28 percent (= .66 x .40-.42), or to somewhat below the prerecession level. Availability of FSB reduced the rate still further. The FSB data in table V.3 indicate an exhaustion rate for that program of about 60 percent. Hence it appears that with the FSB paid during the recession of the mid 1970's, only about 16-17 percent (= .26-.28 x .6) of those individuals who received a first payment under the regular state UI program during the period remained unemployed sufficiently long so as to exhaust all benefits. FSB reduced the final exhaustion rate to well below its full employment level.

TABLE V.3

Annual Program Data for EB and FSB, 1974-1977

Year	EB Program			FSB Program		
	First Payments (Thousands)	Final Payments (Thousands)	Final ÷ First Payments	First Payments (Thousands)	Final Payments (Thousands)	Final ÷ First Payments
1974	915	468	--	--	--	--
1975	4012	2477	--	2661	1212	--
1976	3253	2405	--	2218	1500	--
1977	2656	1761	--	1176	909	--
Total, 1974-77	10836	7111	0.66	6055	3621	0.60

SOURCE: Data for EB from *Handbook of Unemployment Insurance Financial Data,* U.S. Department of Labor, Employment and Training Administration, Unemployment Insurance Service. Data for FSB from special tabulations provided by the Unemployment Insurance Service.

Another way of estimating the impact of FSB on the final exhaustion rate for UI uses statistical regression techniques. In a case study of Pennsylvania and Georgia, Hight (1975) found that the final exhaustion rate for UI could be kept relatively constant by a policy of increasing potential durations by about 4-5 weeks for each 1 percentage point increase in the insured unemployment rate (IUR) above 4 percent.[4] Since, as previously shown, the IUR reached a maximum of about 6.5 percent (on a seasonally adjusted basis) during the recession, an increase of 12-13 weeks of potential benefits (approximately what was provided by EB) would have kept the final exhaustion rate relatively constant, according to the Pennsylvania and Georgia analyses. The larger increases resulting from implementation of FSB would presumably have reduced that rate.

Similar results using aggregate data from all 50 states were estimated by Nicholson and Corson (1978). They found that the positive effect on exhaustions of a 1 percentage point increase in the IUR could be offset by a 15 percent increase in average potential durations. (This calculation disregards any disincentive effects that may arise from increases in potential durations. Such effects were discussed in the previous chapter.) Hence, the impact of the rise in the IUR from 3.5 percent prior to the recession to 6.5 percent at its height could have been offset by roughly a 50 percent expansion in potential durations, which is about the expansion that was provided under the regular EB program. The Nicholson-Corson results suggest that the additional duration provided by FSB (over and above that from EB) should have reduced final exhaustion rates to about half the level they would have been in the program's absence—a finding generally consistent with similar estimates provided from the program data.

---

4. The IUR reflects regular UI claims only.

FSB Compensation for Earnings Losses

The argument presented above implicitly assumes that the exhaustion rate is an appropriate measure of whether UI is providing protection during recessionary periods similar to the protection provided during normal periods. An alternative and more comprehensive measure of protection is provided by the "earnings replacement rate"—that is, the ratio of all UI benefits received during the period of unemployment to the after-tax earnings losses suffered during that period. We examine this measure of protection with the purpose of identifying how durations must be adjusted to keep average earnings replacement rates roughly comparable between recessionary and nonrecessionary periods. The average earnings replacement rate can be expressed as a weighted average of the mean earnings replacement rates of exhaustees and nonexhaustees.[5]

$$r = (1\text{-}p)\ \mathrm{WRR} + p \cdot \mathrm{WRR}\left(\frac{D}{S}\right)$$

where:

r = expected replacement rate
p = probability of benefits exhaustion
D = potential benefits duration for typical claimant
S = unemployment duration for exhaustees

WRR = UI weekly benefit amount divided by after-tax earnings on the pre-UI job.

To understand how this equation works it may be helpful to consider a few examples. First, consider a claimant who

5. This formulation ignores the waiting week but that omission does not affect our results substantially. The appendix to this chapter presents results that take account of the waiting week.

does not expect to exhaust his or her benefits. Then p = 0, and r and WRR are identical (say approximately 0.6 for typical claimants). For an individual with the same WRR who has a 50 percent probability of exhausting his or her benefits, the computation also requires knowledge of the expected total weeks of unemployment. Suppose S = 39 for exhaustees and that D = 26. Then r can be calculated to be 0.5 [= .5 x .6 + .5 x .6 x (26/39)]. In our analysis of the equation, we assume that its various components take on their average values in the population. We are therefore analyzing the situation of a typical claimant.

We expect that both the probability of exhaustion and unemployment duration are functions of the unemployment rate and UI potential duration. An examination of the expression shows, as we would expect, that if the exhaustion rate increases, the expected replacement rate drops. Furthermore, if we increase potential duration sufficiently so as to hold the exhaustion rate constant during a recession, the replacement rate may still drop if the ratio of potential UI duration to actual unemployment duration of exhaustees declines. This may well be the typical case in a recession when duration of unemployment tends to be much longer than normal. Thus, holding exhaustion rates constant (as described previously) may not hold the earnings replacement rate constant.

To examine this relationship in more detail we can calculate what change in potential duration will maintain a constant earnings replacement rate for an individual when unemployment rates rise. In the Appendix to this chapter we show that a 1 percentage point rise in the insured unemployment rate can be offset by a 5.1 week rise in the potential duration of UI benefits. Furthermore, we show that if potential durations are increased only enough to keep the exhaustion rate constant, the earnings replacement rate will drop slightly (less than one-half a percentage point). By this criterion, potential duration should have been increased during the recession of the mid 1970s by about 15-18 weeks because the IUR rose about 3.0 to 3.5 points during that period. That is, EB benefits alone were not quite enough to keep average earnings replacement rates constant, but the addition of up to 26 weeks of FSB (in addition to 13 weeks of EB) was too much. One additional 13-week extension (or less) through FSB would have been more than sufficient to provide individuals laid off during the recession with earnings replacement rates similar to those of individuals laid off prior to the recession.

Hence, whether FSB was "necessary" in order for the UI system to continue to provide protection to unemployed workers against earnings losses resulting from the recession similar to what is available during nonrecessionary periods remains a difficult question. Clearly, the incidence of long term unemployment increased substantially during the recession and some type of extended benefits program was required if the commitment to provide workers with similar protection for their complete unemployment spells was to be fulfilled. General labor market data suggest that extensions provided under the regular EB program would have been insufficient to meet this need. But such aggregate measures of duration are subject to a number of biases which may overstate the needs of the UI-eligible population for longer UI protection. Data on FSB exhaustions suggest that EB alone might have been sufficient to prevent exhaustion rates from rising during the recession. Of course, even if exhaustion rates were held constant, the absolute number of exhaustees would have increased because of the increase in the total number of UI recipients during the period. EB alone might not have prevented some decline in earnings replacement rates, which our estimates show would have fallen slightly. But that fall could have been offset by extensions of a much smaller magnitude than FSB actually provided.

D. Income Maintenance and Benefit Extensions

A second distributional rationale for FSB relates to the concern that individuals who exhaust regular UI plus EB during a recession will lose their principal source of income and fall below poverty level. By this argument, the only feasible way to maintain above poverty level incomes for these exhaustees is to extend UI benefits. This argument then focuses attention on the lower end of the income distribution and suggests that the adequacy of extended benefits be judged relative to a social standard such as the poverty line rather than relative to an individual's pre-UI earnings or recurrent expenses. The discussion then reflects the blurring of the distinction between UI and welfare (first presented in chapter II) that occurs as longer potential durations are examined.

This antipoverty rationale for UI extensions during recessions is based on two implicit assumptions. First, it is assumed that present income maintenance programs will not provide exhaustees with an income large enough to prevent a substantial increase in the number and proportion of exhaustee households with incomes below the poverty line. Second, it is assumed that the incidence of low incomes among exhaustees will be more severe during a recession. If this were not the case, this argument for UI extensions could be applied to nonrecessionary periods as well.[6] The possibili-

6. In fact, even if the incidence of poverty is higher during recessions, we might argue that if we help poor exhaustees during recessions, we should do the same when there is no recession. Doing this, however, would alter the UI program's insurance orientation on a permanent rather than temporary basis.

ty that the poverty problem among exhaustees is more serious during recessions is based on three additional considerations. First, during recessions other household income (e.g., spouse's earnings) is likely to be lower, which will contribute to a greater incidence of poverty after UI benefits are exhausted. Second, if potential UI durations were extended during recessions to yield exhaustion rates that equalled those of nonrecessionary periods, exhaustees might still be expected to face longer post-exhaustion spells of unemployment than during nonrecessionary periods. In that case, intertemporal equity considerations would suggest extending durations to equalize the overall rate of earnings replacement provided by UI in recessionary and nonrecessionary times. And third, even if post-exhaustion durations of unemployment were unaffected by the recession, we might argue that individuals observed during nonrecessionary periods have a greater voluntary component to their unemployment. Other things equal, the existence of lower reservation wages or smaller UI disincentive effects during recessions would provide some evidence of this and would provide a rationale for further income support. In the next section we examine each of these considerations in the case of FSB.

E. Antipoverty Effects of FSB

In this section we use data from the FSB program to discuss three issues related to the antipoverty argument for emergency benefit extensions. First, we examine whether other income security programs would have provided adequate protection to EB exhaustees. Next, we investigate whether exhaustees are more needy during recessions. Finally, we ask how well FSB actually fulfilled antipoverty goals.

Adequacy of Other Income Security Programs

Tables V.4 and V.5 show whether other income security programs would have provided adequate protection to EB exhaustees in the absence of FSB. Data in table V.4 show eligibility rates for each of four major means-tested programs that might have provided income to EB exhaustees in the absence of FSB.[7] The data make clear that most families would not have been eligible for any means-tested benefits except food stamps. Considering both the income and asset tests for eligibility, 57 percent of the families would have been eligible for food stamps and only 10 percent eligible for either the regular AFDC program (Aid to Families with Dependent Children) or the AFDC-U (unemployed parent) program. Very few families would have been eligible for Supplemental Security Income (SSI) or means-tested veterans' benefits. The low number of households eligible for AFDC, SSI, and veterans' benefits compared with food stamps derives mostly from the fact that few FSB families fell into the categories of families serviced by these programs, that is, single-parent families with children or two-parent families with an unemployed father or an incapacitated parent (AFDC), the aged (SSI),[8] or veterans with wartime experience (veterans' benefits). For example, only 5 percent of the families met the categorical requirements for regular AFDC and only 10 percent met those for AFDC-U. The Food Stamp Program, on the other hand, has no categorical requirements. The impact of these categorical re-

---

7. A detailed discussion of the method used to compute eligibility and benefits is contained in Corson et al. (1977), appendix 8. An analagous method was used to compute eligibility and benefits for the welfare reform proposal in this chapter.

8. SSI is also available to the blind and disabled; however, it was assumed that FSB recipients, given their past work experience, were unlikely to meet the SSI requirements for blindness or disability. This assumption was also used in the eligibility calculations for the welfare reform proposal that is described below.

TABLE V.4

Percentages of FSB Households Eligible for Benefits Under Selected Transfer Programs if Unemployment Compensation Had Not Been Available (15 State Survey, 1975-77)

Transfer Programs	Percentage of FSB Recipients Eligible for Program
Aid to Families with Dependent Children (AFDC)	
Categorically Eligible	
AFDC Regular	5.4%
AFDC-U	10.1
Income Eligible (AFDC and AFDC-U Combined)	12.3
Income and Asset Eligible (AFDC and AFDC-U Combined)	9.7
Supplemental Security Income	
Categorically Eligible	10.2
Income Eligible	5.2
Income and Asset Eligible	3.5
Food Stamps	
Income Eligible	64.8
Income and Asset Eligible	56.8
Means-Tested Veterans' Benefits	
Categorically Eligible	2.0
Income Eligible	1.4
Weighted Sample Size[a]	6,316

SOURCE: Corson et al. (1977), Table IV.5.

NOTE: "Categorically Eligible" means that recipients' families fit categories required for program eligibility (e.g., that they had minor children in the household). "Income Eligible" means that the family was both categorically eligible and had an income sufficiently low to be eligible for program benefits. "Income and Asset Eligible" means that the family was both income eligible and met asset tests imposed by the program.

a. Sample sizes for computations vary because of incomplete survey data for certain items.

TABLE V.5

Percentage Distribution of FSB Households by Ratio of Income at FSB Start (Assuming Full Utilization of Transfer Benefits) to Poverty Income Level, for Selected Measures of Income[a] (15 State Survey, 1975-77)

Ratio of Household Income to Poverty Line[b]	Income Excludes FSB	Income Includes FSB
0.0-0.5	25.3%	0.6%
0.5-1.0	14.0	16.4
1.0-1.5	18.8	22.2
1.5-2.0	12.6	14.8
2.0-3.0	15.5	21.4
3.0-4.0	8.0	12.6
4.0 and Over	5.8	12.1
Total	100.0%	100.0%
Weighted Sample Size[c]	6,094	5,816

SOURCE: Corson et al. (1977), Table IV.6.

a. All income measures assume full utilization of transfer benefits including the bonus value of food stamps. Income from this latter source is currently not counted in the official U.S. government definition of income.

b. If a ratio of income to the poverty line, calculated to several decimal points, equalled the boundary between two specific class intervals, that observation was assigned to the lower class interval.

c. Sample sizes vary due to incomplete survey data for certain items.

quirements is illustrated most strongly by considering female heads of households in which no male resided. In this case, data (not reported in the table) show that 74 percent of these families were categorically eligible and 70 percent of that total were income and asset eligible for AFDC, yet this latter group accounted for only 5 percent of the total FSB population.

Because AFDC and SSI eligibility imply food stamp eligibility, approximately 13 percent of those on FSB would have been eligible for two or more of the major welfare programs. Thus, very few would have been eligible for more than one program that provides cash or, in the case of food stamps, "near" cash benefits. The bulk of the recipients with low incomes would have been eligible for food stamps only.

Despite these low eligibility rates, it is possible that the programs' benefits might have been concentrated on those with the lowest household incomes, and, therefore, that we might still conclude that extensions of UI were not necessary to maintain incomes at some minimal level. To investigate this issue, we imputed benefits from transfer programs, assuming full utilization by eligible recipients of FSB, and examined the distribution of household income relative to the poverty line at the date of first receipt of FSB. The results are reported in table V.5 for two income distributions. The first excludes FSB from income received at the start of FSB and adds imputed transfers (including the bonus value of food stamps[9]), using the dollar value of transfer benefits that FSB recipients would have been eligible for in the absence of FSB. The second one includes FSB and uses imputed transfers that FSB recipients would have been eligible for while receiving FSB. The data clearly show that, for many households, the current means-tested transfer system would not have maintained household incomes at even a minimal level in the absence of FSB benefits. Thirty-nine percent of the households would have had incomes below the poverty line in the absence of FSB (counting imputed transfers),

9. These data are not comparable to standard government tabulations which do not count any in-kind benefits as income. Food stamps were included here because they are potentially an important income source for the population being examined.

while only 17 percent would have had incomes below poverty while on FSB if all welfare benefits were fully utilized.[10]

The facts that few of the FSB recipients were categorically eligible for cash benefit programs and that UI benefits were usually more generous than AFDC or SSI and food stamps were the main reasons why the current means-tested transfer programs would not have filled the gap in income that would have been left in the absence of an FSB program. Before concluding, however, that this situation will continue to be true in future recessions, we examine the implications of potential changes in the existing welfare system.

Among the most important proposed reforms of the current system is the removal of categorical restrictions on eligibility for benefits. Because these restrictions are one of the main reasons why current means-tested programs do not fill the income gap that would be left if UI were not available, we reexamined this question assuming the Carter Administration's 1977 welfare reform proposal had been enacted (The Program for Better Jobs and Income).[11] This proposal would have replaced the AFDC, SSI, and Food Stamp programs with a federal cash benefit program for all types of families; state supplements for the aged, blind, disabled, and families with children; an expanded Earned Income Tax Credit; and public jobs for adult members of families with children. While such an ambitious, far-reaching program may never be enacted, a reanalysis substituting this program for the current means-tested

10. These comparisons ignore possible behavioral responses by FSB households to the loss of UI benefits. That is, some individuals might have accepted jobs if benefits had not been extended.

11. This analysis is reported in Corson (1978). The Carter proposal is similar to many other recent suggestions and is therefore indicative of the more general issue of how welfare reform might affect the need for emergency extensions.

transfer system shows that 58 percent of the FSB households would have been eligible for one or more of the proposed benefits (cash, tax credit, or a job) in the absence of FSB. A comparison of the effectiveness of this policy proposal in preventing poverty among potential FSB recipients is provided in table V.6. That table shows that, although the incidence of poverty in the absence of FSB is reduced only marginally (from 39 percent to 33 percent) under the welfare reform option, benefits under that program would be concentrated upon the correct households. For example, under this plan 13 percent of the households, compared with 25 percent under the current system, would have had incomes below 50 percent of the poverty line. FSB would still have had an additional antipoverty effect; virtually no households would have had incomes below half the poverty line and only 17 percent would have been below the poverty line. Whether this additional antipoverty effect would be desirable during a future recession is, of course, a political question. However, the data make clear that the antipoverty argument for UI extensions would be less persuasive if a major welfare reform proposal were enacted.

Income Needs for Exhaustees During Recessions

Another assumption underlying the antipoverty argument for FSB-type extensions is that we expect the effect of the loss of UI benefits to be more severe during recessions. Otherwise, the antipoverty argument would apply to nonrecessionary periods as well. As outlined in the previous section, three pieces of empirical evidence could support this hypothesis: available household income might be less during recessions in the absence of UI extensions, post-exhaustion unemployment durations might be longer, and both reservation wages and the disincentive effects of extensions might be smaller during recessions (thereby implying that the long term unemployed were "more deserving").

TABLE V.6

Antipoverty Effectiveness of FSB, Current Welfare System and Welfare Reform Option[a]

Option	Percentage of Households Below Poverty Line	Percentage of Households Below 0.5 Times Poverty Line
No FSB, Current Welfare Program	39%	25%
No FSB, Welfare Reform Option	33%	13%
FSB plus Current Welfare Program	17%	1%

a. Calculations based on data from initial and follow-up FSB surveys.

Unfortunately, little relevant empirical evidence is available on any of these issues. Data on household incomes are available for FSB recipients (at the beginning of FSB) and for a sample of regular UI exhaustees (at the time of exhaustion) in four cities for October-November 1974.[12] Because the regular UI exhaustee sample depleted its benefits just prior to the start of the recession, we could consider it representative of a nonrecession case. A comparison of household income available to this group with that available to the FSB sample in the absence of FSB supports our hypothesis. Thirty-five percent of the regular UI exhaustees had household incomes below the poverty line compared to

12. Details on the regular UI exhaustee study can be found in Nicholson and Corson (1976).

39 percent of the FSB households studied later.[13] The comparable proportions below 1.5 times poverty were 49 and 58 percent, respectively. While these differences are statistically significant, they are not very large and only weakly support the argument that the "need" of exhaustees is greater during recessions.

Empirical evidence for our other two hypotheses is even sparser. Reemployment rates for exhaustees provide an indication of post-exhaustion duration and such rates are available for three recent studies: the four-city study mentioned above, an Arizona study, and a Pennsylvania study (table V.7). Benefit exhaustion in the four-city sample occurred just prior to the start of the recession in 1974, so reemployment rates were probably negatively affected by this recession.[14] The provision of extended benefits two or three months after exhaustion also affected these rates in the same direction. The Arizona sample, on the other hand, exhausted benefits at the end of the same recession (May 1976 to August 1977) and should probably be viewed as a nonrecession sample. Finally, the Pennsylvania data were collected in 1966-67, a nonrecessionary period when unemployment rates were lower than in the 1970s.

Reemployment rates for each of these samples tend to support our hypothesis. Differences in reemployment rates among the three samples are statistically significant and

13. Data for the exhaustee sample are for white recipients only. This group was chosen as more representative of UI recipients in general than the entire exhaustee sample. Its concentration in four cities led to a high proportion of black recipients in the sample. For both exhaustees and FSBs, we have included imputed transfer benefits in income because that measure of poverty status was more readily available. This makes little difference to the comparison.

14. Here we are using data from the four-city exhaustee study as representing the recession case while for the household income comparison we used it as the nonrecession case. The argument for this dual usage is that exhaustion occurred prior to the recession but the post-exhaustion period occurred primarily during the recession.

substantially larger for the nonrecession samples (12 to 17 percentage points higher at the end of 12 weeks). However, this evidence provides only weak support for our hypothesis. The samples are not nationally representative, they were not all drawn at ideal times, and the reemployment rates for the four-city exhaustee sample may have been influenced by the extension of UI as well as by the weak labor market.

TABLE V.7

Percentage of UI Exhaustees Reemployed After Exhaustion of Benefits (Data from Three Sample Surveys)

Weeks Since Exhaustion	Four-City Study (1974-75)	Arizona Study (1976-77)	Pennsylvania Study (1966-67)
2	5.5%	11.5%	--
4	10.5	18.3	24.5
6	14.1	26.4	--
8	16.9	30.2	33.0
10	20.3	37.0	--
12	23.0	40.0	35.5
14	25.2	42.1	--
Sample Size	1054	235	11,511

SOURCE: Data from the four-city study are for whites only and are found in Nicholson and Corson (1976), table V.8. Data for the Arizona study from Burgess and Kingston (1979), table II.7. Data for the Pennsylvania study are reported in Murray (1974).

One final element that would support the hypothesis that UI exhaustees are more needy during recessions than those exhausting benefits during nonrecessionary periods is that unemployment during a recession may have a smaller voluntary component. Other things equal, that hypothesis would be supported if we found lower reservation wages or smaller UI disincentive effects during recessions. We were unable to find any evidence on the cyclical nature of reservation wages, and only one study provides evidence for UI disincentive effects over the business cycle, but it does support our hypothesis. This study (Wandner, 1975) using data on state averages, showed that the disincentive effect of UI benefits as reflected in longer duration of unemployment was smaller in high than in low unemployment years.

Antipoverty Effectiveness of FSB

The empirical evidence presented above, though limited, suggests that the assumptions underlying the antipoverty argument for FSB are essentially correct, i.e., current income maintenance programs do not provide "adequate" incomes for UI exhaustees and their need for income support is probably greater during recessionary periods. Consequently, we should evaluate how well the FSB program fulfilled this antipoverty goal. Two measures of this effect are available. First, at the time of EB exhaustion, 39 percent of the FSB households would have had weekly incomes below the poverty line if FSB had not been extended (see table V.5). With FSB, this figure dropped to 17 percent. Furthermore, with FSB, less than 1 percent had incomes below one-half the poverty line compared with 25 percent without FSB.[15] An alternative way of examining this effect is to consider household income over one year rather than at a given point in time. Data on the distribution of 1975 household income are presented in table V.8 for individuals receiving an FSB first payment in that year. These data show that without FSB 33 percent of the households would have had incomes below

15. These figures overstate somewhat the percentage of households with incomes *above* the poverty line because they assume full utilization of all other transfer benefits.

TABLE V.8

Percentage Distribution of FSB Households by Ratio of 1975 Income to Poverty Income Level, for Selected Measures of Income[a] (15 State Survey, 1975-77)

Ratio of Household Income to Poverty Line[b]	Income Excludes FSB	Income Includes FSB
0.0-0.5	13.2%	6.2%
0.5-1.0	19.3	16.7
1.0-1.5	15.0	17.4
1.5-2.0	13.2	14.5
2.0-3.0	19.7	21.5
3.0-4.0	9.9	12.5
4.0 and Over	9.6	11.3
Total	100.0%	100.0%
Weighted Sample Size[c]	6,769	6,805

SOURCE: Special tabulations from the MPR FSB study data.

a. These income figures exclude the bonus value of food stamps.

b. If a ratio of income to the poverty line, calculated to several decimal points, equalled the boundary between class intervals, that observation was assigned to the lower class intervals.

c. Sample sizes for computations vary because of incomplete survey data for certain items.

poverty level in 1975 if they had made no response to the loss of FSB benefits.[16] With FSB, 23 percent had annual incomes below poverty level. Thus, FSB reduced the incidence of poverty by nearly one-third. This effect varied widely by household type. For example, other data (not reported in the table) show that 36 percent of the households of married male FSB recipients and 18 percent of the households of married female recipients would have had incomes below the poverty standard without FSB. With FSB, the corresponding figures were 23 and 15 percent, respectively.

16. These data include actual but not imputed transfer payments. The bonus value of food stamps was not included in table V.8 tabulations but was included in those presented above. This makes little difference for the comparison.

While the above figures show that the FSB program had a substantial antipoverty effect, the data reported in table V.8 also show that some households would have maintained relatively high incomes without FSB. Almost 40 percent would have had 1975 incomes above two times the poverty level without FSB while 10 percent would have had incomes above four times that level. For a family of four, this represented an annual income in 1975 of about $22,000. Thus, although the FSB program was superior to the available means-tested programs in reducing poverty for UI eligibles, it was target inefficient because a substantial amount of benefits went to the nonpoor.

F. Conclusion

In this chapter we examined two income distributional rationales for the FSB program. The first argued that in order to treat individuals laid off during recessions in the same way as those laid off at other times, UI benefits should be extended because of the longer unemployment durations experienced during recession.

Two measures of this intertemporal equity were examined. First, final exhaustion rates were estimated for the period 1973-78. It was shown that EB alone was sufficient to keep these rates from rising above their pre-recession levels and that the FSB program had the effect of reducing exhaustion rates to about half their pre-recession levels. As a more comprehensive measure of intertemporal equity we introduced the "earnings replacement rate," i.e., total benefits divided by after-tax earnings lost throughout the workers' unemployment. We estimated that to hold earnings replacement rates constant, potential UI duration should be extended by 5.1 weeks for each 1 percentage point increase in the insured unemployment rate. This estimate implies that, during the recession of the mid 1970s, EB benefits alone were not quite enough to keep earnings replacement rates constant, but the addition of 26 weeks of FSB was too much. One emergency 13-week extension (or less) would have been more than sufficient to provide individuals laid off during that relatively severe recession with earnings replacement rates equal to those of individuals laid off in nonrecessionary periods.

The second argument for the FSB program claims that it was needed to prevent the household income of UI exhaustees from dropping below the poverty level. This income maintenance argument assumes that existing means-tested transfer programs would not have provided adequate income support for UI exhaustees and that the need for income support by UI exhaustees was greater during recessionary than during nonrecessionary periods. Available empirical evidence was examined and it suggested that both of these assumptions were correct, although the evidence concerning the second was quite weak. We then examined the antipoverty effectiveness of the FSB program and concluded that FSB benefits had a substantial effect. These benefits reduced the incidence of poverty among FSB households by about one-third. However, this antipoverty effect was target inefficient because substantial benefits were distributed to the nonpoor.

APPENDIX TO CHAPTER V
EARNINGS REPLACEMENT RATE CALCULATIONS

In the body of this chapter we indicated that the total earnings loss replacement rate for an individual was:

$$r = (1\text{-}p)\ WRR + p \cdot WRR \left(\frac{D}{S}\right) \tag{1}$$

where:

r = replacement rate
p = probability of exhaustion of benefits
D = potential duration of benefits
S = unemployment duration contingent on exhaustion of benefits
WRR = UI weekly benefit amount divided by after-tax earnings in the pre-UI job.

We also indicated that p and S were functions of the unemployment rate (u) and potential duration (D).

To investigate the relationship between changes in the replacement rate, the unemployment rate and potential duration we can derive the expression for the differential of r with respect to u and D.

$$dr = \frac{\partial r}{\partial u} du + \frac{\partial r}{\partial D} dD$$

$$= \left[-WRR \frac{\partial p}{\partial u} + WRR \left(\frac{D}{S}\right)\frac{\partial p}{\partial u} - p \cdot WRR\left(\frac{D}{S^2}\right)\frac{\partial S}{\partial u}\right]du$$

$$+ \left[-WRR \frac{\partial p}{\partial D} + WRR\left(\frac{D}{S}\right)\frac{\partial p}{\partial D} + p\frac{WRR}{S} - p \cdot WRR\left(\frac{D}{S^2}\right)\frac{\partial S}{\partial D}\right]dD. \tag{2}$$

If we then ask what change in potential duration (D) will keep the earnings replacement rate constant with an increase in the insured unemployment rate (u) of 1 percentage point, we set $du=1$, $dr=0$, substitute in values for the other variables and compute dD.[1] Estimates for each of these variables are available from prior studies except for S, $\partial S/\partial u$ and $\partial S/\partial D$.[2] Estimates for these parameters can be computed if we assume that the distribution of unemployment spells is an exponential with mean $1/\alpha$. Then it can be shown that $S=D+\frac{1}{\alpha}$. For our calculation we have assumed that the mean duration of unemployment spells is four weeks and hence, $S=30$ weeks. To compute $\partial S/\partial u$ we notice that $\partial S/\partial u=\partial(1/\alpha)/\partial u$. An estimate for this value is 1.2.[3] Finally, $\partial S/\partial D=1+\partial(1/\alpha)/\partial D$ which we have set equal to 1 for the computation. $\partial(1/\alpha)/\partial D$ is the disincentive effect of increasing D and if it were taken into account, D would need to be increased further to keep r constant. Instead, we have assumed that we are not interested in replacing earnings lost because of the disincentive effect and we have set $\partial(1/\alpha)\partial D$ equal to zero.

Using the numbers in the previous paragraph, we find that dD equals 5.1 weeks, i.e., if the IUR rises by 1 percentage point, duration must rise by 5.1 weeks to keep earnings replacement rates constant for individuals.[4] While this number represents our best estimate of dD, the values used in the calculation for some of the parameters are subject to

1. Notice that when $dr=0$, the expression in (2) is independent of WRR.

2. For the calculation we have assumed that $p=.27$ and $D=26$. Values for $\partial p/\partial u$ (.0482) and $\partial p/\partial D$ (-.0139) were computed from a study of exhaustion rates (Nicholson and Corson, 1978, table III.7).

3. In chapter II we reported that the derivative of duration with respect to the unemployment rate was .93. This can be converted to the derivative of duration with respect to the insured unemployment rate by multiplying by 1.33 (See Nicholson and Corson, 1978, page 106).

4. Note that the aggregate compensation rate would not be equalized because WRR changes as the mix of the unemployed changes.

error. In particular, alternative estimates were available for ∂p/∂u and ∂S/∂u.[5] Table V.A.1 reports values for dD for a range of estimates of ∂p/∂u and ∂S/∂u. These estimates range from 4.2 to 7.3 weeks. While this range is fairly large it does not substantially affect the conclusion reached in the chapter—namely, that FSB overcompensated for the effects of the recession. Finally, the calculations presented above ignore the effect of the UI waiting week on the earnings replacement rate. To include this, the first term in the expression for r should be multiplied by (D/(D + 1)). If this is done, two terms are added to the expression for the differential of r and the resulting estimate for dD is raised slightly to 5.4 weeks.

TABLE V.A.1

Alternative Estimates of the Required Change in Weeks of Potential Duration[a]

			∂p/∂u	
		.0275	.0375	.0475
	1.2	4.2	4.6	5.1
∂S/∂u	1.6	5.2	5.6	6.1
	2.1	6.5	6.9	7.3

a. Entries show the increase in weeks of potential duration required to keep the earnings replacement rate constant in response to a one percentage point increase in the insured unemployment rate.

Another possibility is to compute what happens to the earnings replacement rate if the exhaustion rate is held constant when du = 1. This can be computed by noticing that

5. Alternative estimation techniques used in the exhaustion rate study provided estimates for ∂p/∂u that ranged from .0275 to .0475. The .0475 estimate was selected as the best because the effect of the state UI system on the measurement of the IUR was controlled for best in the regression that produced the .0475 estimate. For FSB recipients ∂S/∂u was estimated to be 2.1 for males. The 1.2 estimate was chosen as better because it was derived from a regression on all unemployed individuals, not just those experiencing long unemployment spells.

$dp = (\partial p/\partial u)du + (\partial p/\partial D)dD$ and substituting this in equation (2). When $du = 1$ and $dp = 0$ (i.e., the exhaustion rate is constant), $dD = 3.5$ and we get

$$dr = -\ p\ (WRR)\ (D/S^2)\ (\partial S/\partial u)$$

$$+ 3.5 \left[p\ (WRR/S) - p\ (WRR)\ (D/S^2)\ (\partial S/\partial D) \right] . \qquad (3)$$

If we assume $WRR = .65$ and keep the same values for the other variables, we find that $dr = -.003$ when the exhaustion rate is held constant. That is, a policy that held exhaustion rates constant during recessions would have resulted in a fall in the earnings replacement rate of .003 (i.e., 0.3 percent) for each 1 percentage point increase in the IUR.

VI. UI EXTENSIONS IN FUTURE RECESSIONS

A. Introduction

In the previous chapters we examined experience with the FSB program in the recession of the mid 1970s and evaluated its allocational and distributional effects. We now consider how this experience might be applied during a future recession. The discussion is organized around several policy questions that concern the timing, duration, benefit levels, financing, and other aspects of an FSB program. In conclusion, we discuss some alternatives to FSB-type programs.

B. When Should an FSB-Type Program Be Enacted?

The answer to this question depends to a large extent on the primary rationale for extending benefits during a recession. If the primary aims of such an extension are to compensate individuals for the increase in unemployment durations and to treat these individuals in the same way as individuals laid off during nonrecession periods (that is, keep the probability of exhausting all UI benefits about the same), the current EB program would be sufficient if the recession were relatively mild. For example, the automatic extensions mandated under the EB program would keep exhaustion rates from rising above their pre-recession levels if the rise in the insured unemployment rate remained below 3 percentage points. Alternatively, if policy makers wished to keep earnings replacement rates[1] constant instead of exhaustion rates, EB would be sufficient if the rise in the insured unemployment rate were less than about 2.5 points.[2]

If, instead, the primary rationale for an FSB program is to help prevent a rise in the incidence of poverty among the unemployed, an FSB program might be enacted that would provide lower exhaustion rates or higher earnings replacement rates than would normally result. That is, an FSB program might be enacted in relatively mild as well as relatively severe recessions. The available empirical evidence, however, only weakly supports the notion that the need for an income maintenance oriented FSB program is greater during recessions.

Finally, even if the judgment is made that indicators suggest a recession severe enough to warrant an FSB-type program, there are good reasons for avoiding premature implementation. EB provides some breathing room: individuals who are just exhausting regular benefits when the recession begins can receive up to 13 weeks of added protection from EB; and those who are just being laid off at that time can collect as many as 39 weeks of benefits in all. There is thus sufficient time between the beginning of a recession and the time when its first "victims" would reach FSB to think carefully about whether and how FSB should be provided.

---

1. The earnings replacement rate is defined as the sum of UI benefits divided by after-tax earnings losses experienced over the entire period of unemployment.

2. The IUR rose about three points during the 1974-75 period so some small extension beyond EB would have been appropriate at that time.

C. What Should Be the Duration of an FSB Program?

The answer to this question is similar to that of the previous one. If the rationale for the program is primarily insurance against wage loss, UI durations should be increased about 3.5 to 5.1 weeks for every 1 percentage point rise in the insured unemployment rate above the level for which the EB program is considered satisfactory. A 3.5-week increase would maintain constant exhaustion rates and a 5.1-week increase would maintain constant earnings replacement rates. Such actions would therefore provide UI recipients with similar protection during recessionary and nonrecessionary periods. This strategy implies that an FSB program would only be required during relatively severe recessions and, for most of these, the program need only be of relatively short duration.[3]

Another rationale for an FSB program is a welfare one (i.e., to prevent a rise in the incidence of poverty), and it weakly supports a somewhat longer extension program. We showed in chapter V that existing welfare programs would not have provided an adequate substitute for FSB for low-income households and that there was some weak evidence that the incidence of poverty of UI exhaustees was greater during a recession. No guidance, however, was provided as to how long such a program should last. This is a policy decision and requires an assessment of the trade-off between the increased income support, target inefficiency, and increased work disincentives of UI extensions.

3. Perhaps the goals of FSB-type extensions could be achieved by having a variable number of weeks of EB benefits triggered more or less automatically in response to labor market conditions.

D. Can the Disincentive Effects of UI Extensions Be Mitigated?

Evidence was presented in chapter IV showing that each additional week of potential FSB added at least .1 weeks to the average duration of unemployment because of increased disincentives to take jobs. In the context of the 1974-75 recession, this means that the FSB program added about one-half point to the national unemployment rate. Several suggestions have been proposed about ways in which these disincentives might be mitigated if a decision were made during a future recession to institute an FSB-type program. For example, it may not be desirable merely to extend benefits for all EB exhaustees. Additional eligibility requirements might be considered to reduce the cost of extensions and to try to reduce the disincentive effects of the additional weeks of UI benefits by focusing extensions on those workers with a demonstrated strong work attachment. For example, one suggestion is to limit benefits to individuals who have evidence of substantial pre-layoff work experience.[4] Data from a simulation of the effects of several such policies on the characteristics of FSB recipients are presented in table VI.1. These data focus on variables which may provide some indirect evidence of reduced work disincentive effects. The two demographic variables, sex and age, are used because disincentive effects may vary across such groups, being greater for females and for older individuals. The net weekly wage replacement rate is reported because of the positive effect of weekly wage replacement rates on unemployment duration. The proportion of recipients with a working spouse is reported because this variable may be positively

4. Another rationale for this restriction is that this group should be given greater insurance than individuals with little work experience and this already occurs in the variable duration states.

related to disincentive effects, and finally, labor force status in March 1975 is reported as an indicator of post-unemployment labor force attachment. The data reported in Table VI.1 show that each of the four simulated additional eligibility requirements would have reduced FSB caseloads and cost, but would have had little effect on any of the other reported variables and, presumably, little effect on disincentives. Three of these potential eligibility screens required base period work experience for FSB in excess of that required for regular UI and the fourth screen does not permit individuals who had exhausted EB prior to the implementation of FSB to receive benefits. Because some of these latter individuals had relatively long gaps between EB exhaustion and FSB receipt, it was thought that the principal effect of FSB on their behavior was only to draw many of them back into the labor force in order to collect FSB benefits. In any event, eligibility screens based on work experience seem unlikely to reduce the disincentive effects of FSB.

A final simulated policy, whose results are reported in table VI.1, was to subject FSB benefits to the federal income tax. The principal effect of this was to reduce the net weekly wage replacement ratio from 65 to 60 percent and to reduce the proportion of recipients with a replacement rate above 60 percent from 52 to 42 percent. While in theory such a reduction might help mitigate the disincentive effect of increased duration, empirical tests of this effect with the FSB sample produced statistically insignificant results.

In addition to these policies that would restrict eligibility and benefits for FSB, one policy approach that might reduce the work disincentive effects of UI extensions would be to impose stronger job search and job acceptance requirements on these recipients. This approach was adopted, in fact, during the latter part of the FSB program. Public Law 95-19,

TABLE VI.1

Simulated FSB Program and Recipient Characteristics Under Alternative FSB Eligibility Criteria and Application of the Federal Income Tax

Program Measure and Recipient Characteristic	Actual Experience Under 1975 FSB Program	Alternative Eligibility Requirement[a]: 30 Weeks in Base Year	40 Weeks in Base Year	60 Weeks in 3-Year Base	Not in FSB Backlog	Subject Benefits to Fed. Income Tax
Caseload, as percentage of 1975 program	100.0	76.3	63.5	82.8	85.7	100.0
Cost as percentage of 1975 program cost[b]	100.0	79.7	67.7	85.8	83.8	86.5
Mean Age (years)	38.9	39.7	39.4	40.0	38.4	38.9
Percentage male	52.5	53.0	52.1	55.3	52.9	52.5
Percentage of net wage replaced by UI						
0-40	15.1%	13.9%	13.9%	14.8%	14.6%	19.1%
40-60	33.0	32.7	31.3	33.4	33.3	39.2
60 and over	51.9	53.4	54.8	51.8	52.1	41.7
Total	100.0%	100.0%	100.0%	100.0%	100.0%	100.0%
Mean	64.6	65.0	65.3	65.6	64.7	59.5

Percentage with earning spouse	37.0	37.1	39.0	36.6	37.3	37.0
Labor Force status, March 1976						
Employed	31.2%	31.4%	33.6%	31.8%	31.7%	31.2%
Unemployed	46.7	48.1	45.8	48.0	48.0	46.7
Not in labor force	22.7	20.5	20.6	20.2	20.3	22.7
Total	100.0%	100.0%	100.0%	100.0%	100.0%	100.0%
Weighted Sample Size[c]	6,825	5,207	4,146	5,651	5,849	6,280

SOURCE: Special tabulations based on the MPR FSB study data.

a. "Weeks" refers to weeks of work.

b. For the income taxation option, cost includes an adjustment for additional taxes collected.

c. Sample sizes vary both because of eligibility restrictions and because of incomplete survey data for certain items.

enacted in April 1977, continued the FSB program and, among other provisions, required states to apply a uniform set of job search and job acceptance requirements instead of adopting the state requirements that otherwise applied. These federal requirements disqualified for the duration of their unemployment spell FSB claimants who (1) failed to accept suitable work; (2) failed to apply for suitable work to which they were referred by the state; or (3) failed to seek work actively. These requirements were generally more stringent than those in the regular state programs.[5]

One analysis of the effect of these requirements found that they had a substantial effect on the level of disqualifications, increasing the total by 78 to 287 percent in selected states.[6] Most of these disqualifications were for "not able to" or "not available for" work, but the rate for refusal of suitable work also rose. The effect varied by state, being smallest in those states with eligibility and disqualification provisions in the regular UI program similar to those imposed on FSB. Thus, stiff job search and job acceptance requirements for UI extensions raise the rate of disqualifications and potentially may help mitigate the problem of work disincentives although the connection between disqualification and work disincentives, if any, is not well documented.

E. How Could FSB Benefits Be Targeted More Effectively on the Poor?

If a major goal of future extensions is to prevent increased poverty among UI exhaustees, we have shown in chapter V that it is inefficient to extend benefits to all exhaustees. Some

5. The definition of suitable work in this provision was broader than that used in the regular state programs, including, for example, low wage (i.e., minimum wage) jobs that would not usually be considered suitable for most claimants under the state laws.

6. These results were reported in Felder and West (1978) and Felder and Pozdena (1978).

targeting of benefits to the poorest recipients may be desirable. The effect of several possible methods of doing this are reported in table VI.2. For each method, two measures of effectiveness are reported in addition to the impact on cost and caseload: the net wage replacement ratio and the distribution of program *benefits* by recipients' poverty status. This distributional measure differs somewhat from the concept used in chapter V where the distribution of *recipients* by poverty status was reported. It was chosen to show exactly how FSB expenditures would have been distributed under the various policy options.

The first policy analyzed in table VI.2 is the restriction of FSB eligibility to recipients who, at the time of application, had a household income below the Bureau of Labor Statistic's 1975 lower living standard (i.e., about 1.8 times the poverty line). This policy would have had only a small effect on wage replacement ratios but would have significantly changed the distribution of FSB benefits. Almost 90 percent of program benefits would, under this option, have been paid to recipients with annual incomes below two times the poverty line, compared with the 64 percent paid under the actual 1975 program.[7] A second policy option—subjecting FSB benefits to the federal income tax—would have reduced wage replacement ratios but would have had little effect on the distribution of after-tax benefits. The last two options, reducing the weekly UI benefit by 15 or 25 percent of the sum of the spouse's earnings and the family's rent, interest and dividend income, would have reduced wage replacement rates considerably and shifted the distribution of benefits to lower income households. However, this shifting would not

7. Because poverty measures are based on 1975 annual income but FSB eligibility is based on income at the time of FSB application, some individuals with 1975 household incomes above the lower living standard were still eligible for FSB.

TABLE VI.2

Actual FSB Program Experience and Simulated Experience Under Alternative Policy Options for Eligibility and Treatment of Benefits

FSB Program Measure	Actual Experience Under 1975 FSB Program	Simulated Experience Under Policy Options: Household Income Eligibility-Below 1975 Lower Living Standard[a]	FSB Benefits Subject to Federal Income Tax	Weekly Benefit Reduction by Percent of Other Income: 15 Percent	25 Percent
Recipients eligible as percentage of 1975 program	100.0	69.4	100.0	97.0	89.6
Total cost as percentage of 1975 program	100.0	70.2	86.5[b]	85.5	78.7
Percentage distribution of recipients by ratio of weekly UI benefit to net wage					
0-40	15.1%	16.9%	19.1%	30.1%	34.8%
40-60	33.0	35.3	39.2	36.9	33.8
60 and over	51.9	47.8	41.7	32.9	31.4
Total	100.0%	100.0%	100.0%	100.0%	100.0%
Mean	64.6	62.3	59.5	52.6	50.3

Percentage distribution of FSB outlays by recipients' 1975 household income, excluding FSB, as multiple of poverty level					
0.0-0.5	17.1%	23.3%	16.8%	19.8%	21.4%
0.5-1.0	19.4	27.3	20.2	22.1	23.6
1.0-1.5	14.5	21.0	14.8	15.8	16.4
1.5-2.0	13.1	16.9	13.2	13.2	12.9
2.0-3.0	17.8	9.8	17.7	16.0	14.7
3.0-4.0	9.1	1.4	8.7	7.0	5.8
4.0 and over	9.0	0.3	8.7	6.2	5.3
Total	100.0%	100.00%	100.0%	100.0%	100.0%
Weighted Sample Size[c]	6,806	4,427	6,280	6,723	6,723

SOURCE: Special tabulations from the MPR FSB study data tape.

a. Annual 1975 household income-excludes FSB. The Lower Living Standard is defined by the Bureau of Labor Statistics and is approximately 1.8 times the poverty level.

b. Benefits less applicable income taxes.

c. Sample sizes vary because of eligibility requirements and because of incomplete survey data for certain items.

have been as large as that accomplished with the lower living standard income eligibility screen.

Choosing among these options is difficult because allocational, distributional and administrative goals may be in conflict. The taxing option would be the easiest administratively because the UI system would not need to collect additional data (i.e., income data) to determine FSB eligibility, or to calculate payments as it would for the other options. However, this policy would not significantly affect the distribution of benefits. Of the other two types of policies, the income eligibility screen would probably be the easiest to administer because there would be no question of recalculating the benefit periodically (to account for changes in family income) and because precise measurement of income would only be necessary for individuals near the eligibility cut-off. However, this absolute cut-off of benefits would create incentives for those with incomes above the cut-off line to reduce the spouse's earnings to ensure UI eligibility. Despite this problem, use of an income eligibility screen appears to be the easiest and most effective way for FSB benefits to be targeted to the poor.

F. Can FSB-Type Programs Improve Job Search Outcomes?

Analysis of data from the FSB program showed that FSB recipients who ultimately became reemployed suffered a substantial loss in their real weekly earnings. Weekly wages on jobs held in November of 1977 (about three years after the initial layoff) were, on average, about 10 percent lower in real terms than weekly wages on the pre-UI job. This loss occurred for both real hourly earnings, which declined about 3 percent, and for hours worked, which declined about 6 percent. This average loss masked considerable variation in individual experiences; nearly one-third had jobs paying less (in real terms) than 75 percent of the pre-UI wage. Thus, there are good reasons to ask if these job search outcomes could be improved in future recessions.

Unfortunately, analysis of the reemployed FSB recipients' interview responses also provided little guidance for improving these outcomes. No evidence was found supporting the hypothesis that increased UI durations led to increased post-unemployment wages, and for men, services (such as counseling or job search assistance) provided by the Employment Service (ES) appeared to have had no effect. On the other hand, women who were similarly served by the ES were found to have gained higher weekly wages. For women's hourly wages, however, the effect was insignificant, suggesting that the ES may have helped women obtain full-time rather than part-time jobs.

With regard to training and education, the analysis showed that FSB recipient skill levels were roughly comparable to those of EB recipients. Hence, their long unemployment spells were probably due mainly to the high unemployment rates during the recession, rather than to a substantial lack of job skills. There was little evidence that those enrolled in education or training programs experienced substantial payoffs as a result of their participation. Consequently, the FSB experience sheds little light on the issue of whether training programs should play a role in future emergency extensions.

G. How Should Emergency Extended Benefits Programs Be Financed?

The FSB program was funded in two ways. Until April 1977, costs were charged to the extended unemployment compensation account in the federal unemployment trust fund to which a portion of federal UI tax revenues is allocated. Following that date, the costs were charged to general revenues. The financing of future FSB programs should, in our view, continue to be from general revenues. This method of financing would treat FSB in the same way as other federal countercyclical programs and emphasize that severe national recessions are a federal responsibility. Such a method for financing extensions would result in costs being spread generally over the population rather than being charged to employers only.

That approach is consistent with the notion that long unemployment spells during a recession result from macroeconomic factors rather than from the decision processes of firms. Although general revenue financing of FSB, rather than employer payroll tax financing, may lessen the incentive for firms to recall their own workers, we do not believe this is particularly important for the case of the long-term unemployed.

H. What Alternatives to FSB Are Available?

If, in the future, the nation is faced with a recession severe enough to warrant consideration of an FSB-type program, two alternative programs might also be considered. First, if the principal goal of an FSB-type program is income maintenance for the long term unemployed, then a program based on a household income eligibility test may be appropriate. As we showed in chapter V, the current welfare programs would not provide an adequate income to most UI exhaustees because of categorical eligibility restrictions. But an expanded, more generous welfare system might alter that result.

For example, we showed that the Carter Administration's 1977 welfare reform plan would have halved the proportion of FSB recipients under the 1975 program with household incomes below one-half the poverty level. An FSB program would, in this case, have an additional antipoverty effect, but the income maintenance argument for FSB-type extensions would be less strong than is presently the case.[8]

A public service employment program (PSE) for UI exhaustees might also be considered as a potential substitute for FSB extensions. While the choice between these two programs is partly one of congressional preference, several points in favor of FSB extensions can be raised. First, starting up a major PSE program would probably take longer, thus its impact might be delayed relative to that of FSB extensions. Second, phasing out a PSE program may be more difficult than phasing out an FSB program, particularly since any time limit placed on PSE jobs is likely to be longer than any placed on FSB benefit extensions. Third, the cost of a PSE job slot is probably higher than the cost of FSB benefits paid to the individual, given that the value of output from PSE jobs may be low and given the relatively sizable rate of substitution for PSE jobs.[9] Fourth, any argument for PSE that emphasizes the training aspect of employment may not be particularly important for UI exhaustees because most already have substantial job experience and skills. And finally, it may not be possible to create PSE jobs on a scale that would equal the scale of FSB-type programs and any attempt to do so would likely exacerbate the timing problems

8. Another alternative would be (as described in table VI.2) to apply some sort of reduction in benefits for a portion of other income. Income tested unemployment assistance was recommended by the National Commission on Unemployment Compensation (1980) p. 172, although it also recommended FSB extensions.

9. For a discussion of these issues see Garfinkel and Palmer (1978), pages 6-11. "Substitution" occurs when PSE funds are used to finance ongoing local municipal employment rather than to create new jobs.

mentioned above. Thus, in future recessions, PSE jobs are likely to be only a partial substitute for FSB extensions, if they are judged necessary at all.

REFERENCES

Barron, J.M., and W. Mellow. "Search Effort in the Labor Market." *Journal of Human Resources* 14 (Summer 1979): 389-404.

Becker, Joseph M. *In Aid of the Unemployed.* Baltimore: Johns Hopkins University Press, 1965.

Brewster, J. Alan, Walter Corson, John Friedmann, Walter Nicholson, and Andrea Vayda. *Final Report, Follow-up Study of Recipients of Federal Supplemental Benefits.* MPR Project Reports Series 78-15. Princeton: Mathematica Policy Research, Inc., 1978.

Burgess, Paul L. and Jerry L. Kingston. *Labor Market Experiences of Unemployment Insurance Exhaustees.* Unemployment Insurance Occasional Paper 79-3. U.S. Department of Labor, 1979.

Burns, Eveline M. *The American Social Security System.* Boston: Houghton Mifflin Company, 1949.

Clague, Ewan. "Social Security in a Stable Economy." Discussion in the *Papers and Proceedings of the American Economic Association,* January 1949.

Classen, Kathleen P. "The Effect of Unemployment Insurance on the Duration of Unemployment and Subsequent Earnings." *Industrial and Labor Relations Review* 30 (July 1977): 438-44.

Corson, Walter, David Horner, Valerie Leach, Charles Metcalf, and Walter Nicholson. *Final Report, A Study of Recipients of Federal Supplemental Benefits and Special Unemployment Assistance.* MPR Project Reports Series 77-01. Princeton: Mathematica Policy Research, Inc., 1977.

Corson, Walter. "Preliminary Draft, Welfare Reform and Extension of Unemployment Compensation Benefits." Princeton: Mathematica Policy Research, Inc., June 1978.

Crosslin, Robert. "Unemployment Insurance and Job Search." Mississippi State University, Department of Economics, 1975. (Mimeographed.)

Ehrenberg R. G. and R. L. Oaxaca. "Unemployment Insurance, Duration of Unemployment and Subsequent Wage Gain." *American Economic Review* 66 (December 1976).

Felder, H. and R. Pozdena. *The Federal Supplemental Benefits Program: Impact of P.L. 95-19 on Individual Recipients.* Unemployment Insurance Occasional Paper 78-4, U.S. Department of Labor, 1978.

Felder, H. and R. West. *The Federal Supplemental Benefits Program: National Experience and the Impact of P. L. 95-19.* Unemployment Insurance Occasional Paper 78-1, U.S. Department Labor, 1978.

Garfinkel, Irwin and John Palmer. "Issues, Evidence and Implications," in John Palmer, ed. *Creating Jobs, Public Employment Programs and Wage Subsidies.* Washington, D.C.: The Brookings Institution, 1978.

Hamermesh, Daniel. *Jobless Pay and the Economy.* Baltimore: Johns Hopkins University Press, 1977.

Hight, Joseph E. "Insured Unemployment Rates, Extended Benefits and Unemployment Insurance Exhaustions." *Proceedings of the Industrial Relations Research Association* 28 (December 1975): 242-49.

Holen, Arlene. "Effects of Unemployment Insurance Entitlement on Duration and Its Search Outcome." *Industrial and Labor Relations Review* 30 (July 1977): 445-50.

Kaitz, H.B. "Analyzing the Length of Spells of Unemployment." *Monthly Labor Review* 90 (November 1970): 11-20.

Moffitt, Robert and Walter Nicholson. "The Effect of Unemployment Insurance on Unemployment: The Case of Federal Supplemental Benefits." Paper presented at the Annual Meetings of the Econometric Society, Atlanta, 1979.

Murray, Merrill G. *The Duration of Unemployment Benefits.* Kalamazoo, MI: W.E. Upjohn Institute for Employment Research, January 1974.

National Commission on Unemployment Compensation. Final Report, Washington, D.C., July 1980.

Newton, F. and H. Rosen. "Unemployment Insurance, Income Taxation, and Duration of Unemployment: Evidence from Georgia." *Southern Economic Journal* 45 (January 1979): 773-84.

Nicholson, Walter and Walter Corson. *A Longitudinal Study of Unemployment Insurance Exhaustees.* MPR Project Reports Series 76-01. Princeton: Mathematica Policy Research, Inc., January 1976.

Nicholson, Walter and Walter Corson. *The Effect of State Laws and Economic Factors on Exhaustion Rates for Regular Unemployment Insurance Benefits: A Statistical Model.* Unemployment Insurance Occasional Paper 78-7, U.S. Department of Labor, 1978.

Nicholson Walter and Walter Corson. "The Duration of Unemployment Insurance Benefits over the Business Cycle: A Theoretical and Empirical Analysis." Paper presented at the Second Annual Research Conference, Association for Public Policy Analysis and Management, Boston, October 1980.

Solon, Gary. "Labor Supply Effects of Extended Unemployment Benefits." *Journal of Human Resources* 14 (Spring 1979): 247-55.

VonFurstenberg, G.M. "Stabilization Characteristics of Unemployment Insurance." *Industrial and Labor Relations Review* 29 (April 1976): 363-76.

Walsh, Brendan M. "Unemployment Compensation and the Rate of Unemployment: The Irish Experience," in H.G. Grubel and M.A. Walker, eds. *Unemployment Insurance: Global Evidence of Its Effect on Unemployment.* Vancouver: The Fraser Institute, 1978, pp. 172-201.

Wandner, Stephen. "Unemployment Insurance and the Duration of Unemployment in Periods of Low and High Unemployment." Unpublished paper, Unemployment Insurance Service, U.S. Department of Labor, 1975.